THE CHILD/ADULT SAFETY BIBLE

CORY B. HARRIS, MS

Full operating and publishing rights Sir Bernard Cordell CMD Publishing and Production, LLC. Republished by Sir Bernard Cordell Publishing 08/10/2011

Sir Bernard Cordell CMD Publishing and Production, LLC
P.O. Box 1661
Texarkana, TX 75504

Printed by DiggyPOD 8-3-2011

ISBN: 978-0-615-52513-6

Library of Congress Control Number: 2011903548

Printed in the United States of America

Any people depicted in stock imagery provided by Thinkstock are models, and such images are being used for illustrative purposes only. Certain stock imagery © Thinkstock.

This book is printed on acid-free paper.

Because of the dynamic nature of the Internet, any web addresses or links contained in this book may have changed since publication and may no longer be valid. The views expressed in this work are solely those of the author and do not necessarily reflect the views of the publisher, and the publisher hereby disclaims any responsibility for them.

The word "bible" as used in the title is in no-way intended to offend or disrespect any person or religion.

This book is dedicated to Warren G. Elliott

A fine example of what an honorable and decent man should be. The Lord made very few like him, and he will be missed.

Contents

The author expresses gratitude for the
foreword to this book, written by:

M. Randall Harris, FBI Special Agent (Retired) and

Charla Woodruff, Sex Crimes Investigator

FOREWORD
M. Randall Harris

During my career as an FBI special agent, I was the case agent on numerous investigations where children were the victims of crime. From the drug overdose deaths of teenagers targeted by black-tar heroin dealers, to the purveyors of child pornography, to the sexual molestation of children, I have witnessed my share of the devastating effects crime can have on children and their families. Without question, one of my most memorable cases will be the exhaustive three-year investigation and prosecution of self-proclaimed evangelist Tony Alamo, who is now serving a 175-year federal sentence after his conviction related to the sexual exploitation of young girls in his "ministry."

In a number of these cases, it became apparent that children became vulnerable to those who would prey upon them due to a lack of parental oversight and/or the apathy of other adults who could have, and should have, taken steps to intervene. In the Alamo case, an entire culture of adults turned a blind eye as Alamo took multiple young girls, as young as nine, to be his "brides" and inflicted other forms of physical abuse on the other young girls and boys within the group. In this particular case, it was the children themselves who eventually mustered up the courage to report the abuse. While it is truly important that our children be educated as to the evils which exist in today's fast-paced society, it is equally important that adults be educated as to their responsibilities. Adults should be increasingly vigilant in preventing our children from becoming victims and should be willing to "get involved" when necessary.

I had the opportunity to work with Cory Harris during the last year of my FBI career, and I am pleased that he is carrying on the effort to make our communities a safer place for our most valuable asset, our children.

—M. Randall Harris
Retired FBI Special Agent

FOREWORD
Charla Woodruff

A perfect world would mean our children being completely safe at all times and in whatever circumstances. However, we know that our world is not perfect. In fact, our society has become extremely wicked. The numbers for sexual crimes are constantly on the rise. Our children are continually being put in situations which provide opportunities for them to be hurt physically and emotionally. Without a conscious effort by everyone—parents, grandparents, teachers, law enforcement—the number of victims will never decrease. Education is key in this circumstance. Parents, play an active role in your child's life and talk to your children. Set up guidelines for Internet and social activities. Our role is to also stay aware of what is going on around us.

Cory Harris has worked numerous hours, both on the street and through research, to get these offenders away from our children. Harris has organized and supervised the West Arkansas Fugitive Task Force in my area, through which many offenders who had "slipped through the cracks" and the ones who are attempting to offend through the Internet have been stopped. In Harris's devotion to keeping our children safe, he has stressed education to his local community and law enforcement. Harris's research is shared within these pages, in the form of tips on how not only to create a better and safer household for your family but to make you aware of the society around them and its potential dangers. In creating the Child/Adult Safety Council, Harris has compiled a variety of people from various professions who also have children's best interests at heart. Harris believes that children are our most valuable resource. The goal of this council is to recognize all of the potential dangers for our children, create awareness of them as well as solutions.

As a single mother myself, I recognize the significance of being aware of my surroundings and the situations in which I put my daughter but, more importantly, of teaching her what is appropriate and inappropriate behavior both for herself and for outsiders. She is very young right now, and her safety is totally my responsibility. But it is also my responsibility, as she grows older, to empower her with the knowledge and tools she needs to be responsible about contacts she makes and to keep herself as safe as possible in this wicked world.

—Charla Woodruff
Former Sex Crimes Investigator Miller County Sheriff's Office
Child/Adult Safety Council Member
Mother

INTRODUCTION

According to the National Center for Missing and Exploited Children (NCMEC), after polling individual state sex-offender registries, there were reported to be 602,182 registered sex offenders in the United States as of mid-2007. On average, each year about three thousand to five thousand non-family abductions are reported to police. Unfortunately, many of these are sexually motivated cases, and some end in death for the child who is victimized.

It is obvious to anyone who picks up a newspaper or watches the evening news that there are people out there who seek to harm our children—who are our most precious resource. As a parent, *you* are the best person to protect your child and in the best position to do so. Knowledge is the key to an aggressive defense of what is important to you.

Information is readily available, and there are many people who are eager to help you do what is necessary to keep your child safe. The problem has been that the information is often fragmented and cannot be found all in one place. This book will attempt to bring all the pertinent information to the fingertips of a parent who is interested in child safety. Opinions of experts as well as the latest safety techniques and resources are combined in a single source within the pages of this book.

As an adult parent, you have to be there for your child, meaning you have to be alive and safe to raise your child properly, because again, as a parent no one can protect your child or is in a better position to do so than *you*. Therefore, this book will cover adult safety as well, providing tips and information at the most basic levels. As a result, you may find there is a lot you already know but you may be surprised to find what you *don't* know included also.

The information contained in this book features the opinions and outlook of the author and how he sees certain issues, and is not representative of any agency or organization. The views are independently gained from nearly twenty years' experience in dealing with these issues.

CHAPTER 1

CHILD SAFETY— WHAT RISK DO WE FACE?

Children of every gender, race, and age are vulnerable to child abduction. Every home, school, and preschool *should* teach children some form of safety and protection. However, this is not always the case; you can't always depend on an institution to teach a child everything he or she needs to know. In these cases, it is incumbent upon the parent or guardian to ensure that valuable lessons are taught in regard to child safety.

In order to protect our children from potential danger, we must first identify and understand exactly whom we are protecting them against. A 1992 Justice Department National Survey of Crime Victims found that one-third of all molesters had attacked their own child or stepchild. Another one-half of all molesters were a friend, acquaintance, or more distant relative of their victim. Only one in seven molested a child who was a complete stranger. So many people won't acknowledge the fact that statistically, the individual who is going to hurt your child is a family member or close friend who may have frequent access to your child. When you consider the fact that less than 5 percent of children who are molested will report it to their parents on their own, you can clearly note the potential for danger, additionally if in 1992 one-third of molesters attacked their own child or step child that number may be even higher today.

There is nothing wrong with being suspicious of anyone or anything that comes into contact with your child that doesn't seem quite right. Do not allow yourself to turn a blind eye to certain indicators just because the potential offender is a relative or friend. In many cases, it is just a matter of convenience for an offender; they will often simply violate the child they have the most access to.

Who are the Sex Offenders?

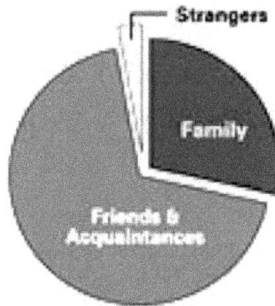

2004 figures for Vermont and New Hampshire combined, in cases where police identified the relationship, about 90 percent of the total.

Terms like *pedophile, predator, sexually violent offenders,* and *incest-based offenders* are commonly used interchangeably, but each has a social, clinical, or legal definition. Let us examine them one by one.

- **Pedophiles**—(A person who is sexually attracted to children, Collins English Dictionary 2009) Adults who have strong interest in and are sexually attracted to prepubescent children. A pedophile is sexually aroused by children but may not ever act on the impulse; however, the desire is there.

Things to note in relation to pedophiles:

— They may work with children or volunteer for work involving children often.

— A pedophile can be anyone. It is commonly believed they are likely to be single, have a dysfunctional marriage, or live with their parents. While this is true for some, it is not an absolute by any means.

— Common belief is that pedophiles are socially inhibited. But be aware: some are extremely charming and use this to gain your trust as well as the child's.

— The target of a pedophile, by clinical definition, is usually pre-pubescent children.

— They may not have a criminal record, because they may never have offended before or been caught offending, in which case they would be classified as a sex offender.

— Statistics show the majority are likely to re-offend.

• **Predators and sexually violent offenders**—This is the group who are more likely to kidnap, rape, and even murder child victims. This is not to say that a pedophile won't resort to violence as well, once they act on their impulses; however, this group constitutes a small but dangerous group of child molesters.

Things to note in relation to predators and violent offenders:

— In addition to a sexual assault, they frequently will assault their victims physically.

— They may assault adults as well, may be unemployed, and have a parasitic lifestyle.

— A criminal history check will usually reveal a lengthy criminal history of various crimes, violations of probation, and failed rehabilitation or treatment.

— For these offenders, the re-offense rate is just as high for generic criminal behavior as it is for their sex crimes.

— The key word in all this is "may." These offenders may not show any of these characteristics but may still be just as dangerous.

— It goes without saying that if your child is abducted by a member of this group, time is critical.

- **Incest-based offenders**—This description includes the word "based" because they prefer to abuse their own children or relatives, whether it be for convenience or personal preference. That does not preclude them from violating children to whom they are not related as well. They may offend because they are simply seeking intimate contact with children and usually fail to understand or care that that they are hurting the child.

Things to note in relation to incest-based offenders:
— They may have no gender preference and will abuse both boys and girls at various ages.

— Most blend into normal society and have no notable or noticeable pathology.

— May have little or no criminal history.

— May prefer to offend inside the family, but will also offend outside the family.

— Skilled in coercion of children and adults; may have been successful at talking victims and family out of reporting the offense when detected.

- **The opportunistic offender**—These offenders will only offend when an easy opportunity presents itself. They may have a lot to lose if they are discovered. This is the primary motivation to control their desires: they strike when they feel they can get away with the crime. This group has a lot in common with the pedophile, but the difference is the opportunistic offender may be even more elusive.

Things to note in relation to the opportunistic offender:
— May have a good career or position of prominence in the community.

— Will be one who has a lot of influence over the child or the parent or both.

— May be a charismatic figure.

— Likely well-liked and respected by all.

— May be stable, married and have children of their own.

As you may have already noted, some of the characteristics we have discussed may fit many people. Even if an individual displays some of the characteristics we discussed, such as living at home with parents or doing lots of volunteer work with children, this does *not* automatically mean they are an offender or a pedophile. The best rule is to be cautious and aware of everyone when it comes to *your* child. This would include family members and friends, since statistically the majority of children are abused by persons known to them.

The facts are just the facts, so no matter how much of a "great guy" an uncle, a distant cousin, or a family friend is, you have to keep in mind that he could be a pedophile or incest-based offender. You never know. There is no need to be rude, but at the same time, don't talk yourself out of your own basic and natural suspicions. ***If it doesn't feel right, it may not be right.*** Your suspicion and awareness are your first line of defense. As a parent, you may occasionally irritate someone who would desire you to trust *them* with *your* child. This is okay; better someone be a little irritated or even angry, as long as your child is alive and well. If you don't feel comfortable with your child riding with another adult to a function or being around a particular person, simply restrict it from happening. You have the power and authority to do so. In many cases, your child's behavior is the best evidence that something may be wrong. In all instances, make note of the following signs if you notice any of them:

• If your child displays a newfound fear of a place they have visited in the past.

• A newfound fear or apprehension of a person they have been around before. This is an especially telltale sign with a family member who may have harmed the child. There are few explanations for why a child would suddenly be uncomfortable around a family member they have been around several times in the past. Be very concerned if your child demonstrates such behavior.

- A recent upsurge in nightmares the child might be having. If you notice this, try to find out the source of the uneasiness.

- Sudden inclusion of genitals in the child's drawings, and awareness of words associated with sex. Depending on the child's age, it is doubtful he or she is aware of many sexually related themes, unless the child has been exposed in some way.

Aside from behavior, also monitor your child physically. You can look for signs of abuse such as bleeding or suspicious injury near the genitals, redness, swelling, and tenderness. Keep in mind that many cases of sexual abuse do not involve actual penetration, so there may be no physical injury. Sex offenders often try to use the lack of physical injury as their proof of innocence. The main indicator will be the child's behavior.

It's possible to have sexual abuse without physical injury, but very unlikely to have sexual abuse without some change in the behavior of the child. A knowledgeable investigator will know this, if a situation is reported to the police, so in your initial observation, weigh the unusual behavior heavily. The body, at some point will likely heal from injuries related to sexual abuse and may hide what has happened, this is why it is important to remember-the most permanent damage, and signs that abuse has occurred will be evident in the mind of the victim. The key is recognition of these signs of damage when and if they manifest themselves

TACTICS OFFENDERS MAY USE TO ACCESS YOUR CHILD

As we have noted, offenders are classified and grouped in part by the way they gain access to their victim. The majority of offenders abuse children they are related to or have regular access to by position as a volunteer, coach, stepparent, mother's boyfriend, uncle, neighbor, babysitter, and so forth. Because of family ties or close relationships due to position, people have a hard time believing these offenders are guilty and fail to be suspicious or report their activity to the police. The sad truth is, everything about an offender could appear totally normal, which is why you have to be a little suspicious of everyone and take the proper precautions.

Offender Methodology

There are several different ways an offender may increase his access to and influence over your child. The most commonly used ones will be included here for discussion. In no way is this discussion exhaustive of all methods an offender may utilize.

An offender will often take a direct approach in attempting to seduce and deceive in a number of ways. The offender may attempt to:

- Impress the child with a glowing personality.
- Buy the child excessive and unwarranted candy or toys.
- Invite the child over to play with toys or video games.
- Show the child excessive unnecessary amounts of affection.
- Attempt to gain background information on the child.
- Ask the child the work hours of their parents.
- Frequently contact the child when parents or other adults are not present.
- Involve himself or volunteer for activities that the targeted child is involved in.

Once the offender has regular access, he will then likely employ even more sophisticated methods. The offender will have to pique the child's interest and keep it that way. The offender may utilize some of the following as a tool. Again, in no way is this a list of everything he could use.

1. Alcohol

2. Cigarettes

3. Illegal narcotics

4. Pornography

5. Blackmail

6. Position of authority

7. Threats

8. Coercion

This is in no way a full list of tools an offender may use; they will simply use whatever is at their disposal that they can play on as an "in." Let's break this list down and look a little closer at the ones we did name, since they are common.

Tool/Vehicle	Gender the child offender may prefer to target	Likely to be used by family member	Likely to be used by stranger/ non-family member	How the tool may be deployed
Alcohol	Both		X	The offender may use as an enticement to lure the victim to a certain location. The draw is making it easier for the victim to get something it may be otherwise difficult to get.
Cigarettes	Male		X	Similar to alcohol, the offender makes it easier to get something that might be otherwise difficult to obtain.
Illegal Narcotics	Both		X	The offender may play on the curiosity of the victim and the impulse to rebel, and implant the idea it is cool to get high.

Pornography	Male	X	X	Used as a seductive method to misrepresent moral standards and stimulate interest. Through this medium, the offender can portray the acts as common or normal.
Blackmail	Both	X	X	Once the child has been compromised, the offender can threaten exposure to gain better control of the victim.
Position of Authority	Both	X	X	The offender already has some influence and simply uses his stature to impose his will on the child.
Threats	Both	X	X	Used to imply negative results to victim's complaints and ensure the victim's continued participation; rarely is a threat of harm actually used.
Coercion	Both	X	X	Used by the charismatic offender to convince the victim that bad is good by making suggestions packaged in the most articulate of ways.

This is not an exact science by any stretch, but there are some things that are common. The methods that offenders use and the race, sex, and type of victim they target can vary greatly from anything you would ever read on the patterns of offenders. This is why the crime these offenders commit can be very difficult to detect and even harder to prevent. Geographically, the odds of a sex offender who has hurt children living within five miles or less is often greater than most people think. This is why the parent or guardian must stay vigilant. No matter how harsh it sounds, trust no one when it comes to your child's safety.

"Trust no one," as it is used in this text, refers most often to blind trust, trust that is unsubstantiated or unfettered. Take special precaution with female children, as studies show that roughly one in five are molested before they are eighteen. Know the likelihood of the enemy would-be offender; only about 10 percent are female. This means that in most cases, the offender who would harm your child will be male.

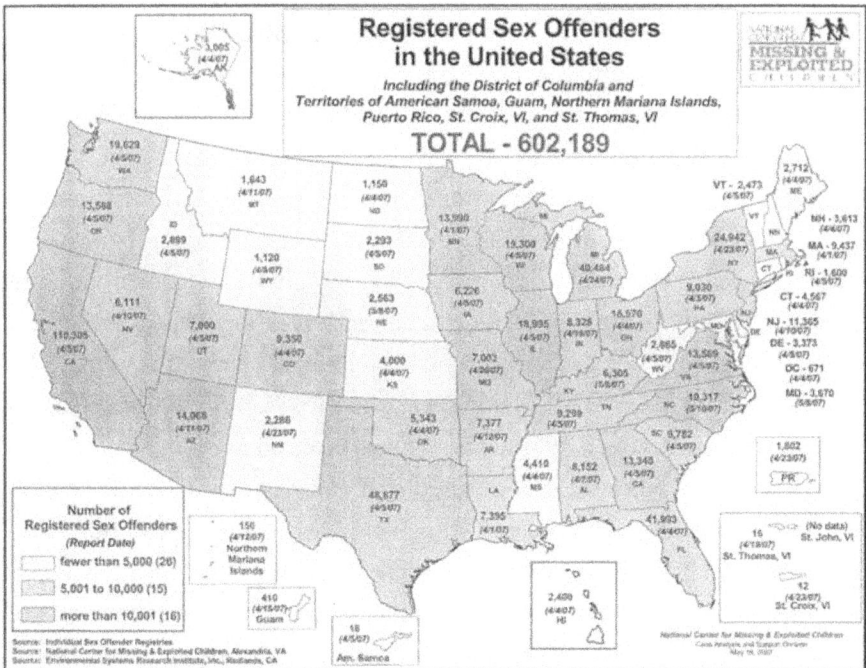

Registered Sex Offenders in the United States

Including the District of Columbia and Territories of American Samoa, Guam, Northern Mariana Islands, Puerto Rico, St. Croix, VI, and St. Thomas, VI

TOTAL - 602,189

In 2007, the National Center for Missing and Exploited Children (NCMEC) showed a total of 602,189 registered sex offenders in the United

States and its territories. This map, of course, is older, and a current one is available on the NCMEC website. We have included it here to serve as a baseline. These numbers have all continued to rise since 2007. At present, the total is closer to seven hundred thousand known registered, and again, those are *only* the ones who have registered.

The key thought here to remember is, this is the number of sex offenders who are actually registered. The total is only a reflection of those offenders who have been caught and exposed for what they are. Often, offenders who are caught have offended multiple times before they are actually caught, and due to the tactics that some use to avoid detection, some are never caught. This simply means that the total number of offenders who are actually in the United States is much higher than the registered 602,189 in 2007.

The US Department of Justice Reports that in a one-year period, 797,500 children younger than 18 were reported missing (Sedlak, Finkelhor, Hammer, Schultz, 2002- U.S. Department of Justice "National Estimates of Missing Children"). This number is alarming and is considerably higher than the number of offenders who are registered.

Offenders who abduct and molest children sometimes do so because they are emotionally attracted to the children they target as victims. In addition, they target children whom they feel need or lack attention, or children who are vulnerable in other ways. They also consider the extent to which they can manipulate or control the victim, in order to keep the abuse a secret. Secrecy is most important to offenders who are pedophiles and opportunists. The key to their success in relation to the abuse they inflict is that it *not* be discovered. The longer something can go undetected, the longer it can continue. Even in cases where the child is abducted, the more time that passes before it is discovered that the child is missing, the more harm can be inflicted before any effort is made to locate the child.

As you may have already noted, there is no single pattern that can be pinpointed in gauging who will or will not hurt children. Nor can you always predict when it will happen, but the more examples you have of how some offenders think and act, the better. The Kenosha (Wisconsin) Police Department once displayed on its website, in the sex offender notification facts, two examples taken directly from a sex offender's treatment summary:

- Many pedophiles seek out mothers of single parent families for the purpose of victimizing their children. As an example, the following was taken directly from a sex offender's treatment summary:

  "During treatment … (Name) … undisclosed- said that he has been sexually assaulting children, males and females, since he was 8 or 9 years old. His victims range in age from 2 to 10 years old. He groomed his victims by keeping candy, popsicles, and children's toys in his apartment. He raised birds to attract children; took children to the park, beach and McDonald's; and used children he was babysitting to gain access to other victims. He groomed the parents by offering free babysitting; helping out by providing transportation and money "when they needed it." He disclosed he gains access by targeting single parents with a large number of children who are not good housekeepers. In his words, "a mother who doesn't give a damn."

- Most sex offenders "groom" their victims prior to any sexual abuse. As an example, the following was taken directly from a sex offender's treatment summary:

  "He played the part of (Name)'s best friend by being around her as much as possible and telling her she could always come to him if she needed someone to talk to. He helped (Name) do her homework and her household chores. He played games with (Name) and took her to the park. Other places he took her were the malls, toy stores, clothing stores, and swimming pools. He gave (Name) money and bought her things, such as new toys, board games, a bike, and expensive clothing. When he was babysitting (Name), he would tell her she could do anything she wanted. He told (Name) if she would let him do what he wanted to her, he would buy her things. To keep her quiet, he told (Name) that if

her mother found out about what "we" were doing, she would be
mad and it would be all (Name)'s fault."

*   *   *

There is another type of victimization that has recently surfaced and
been used against children. If your child has a cell phone, you should
be mindful of several things; one in particular is a blackmail scheme. It
involves an adult male texting a young male or female child. If the child
is a male, the adult simply poses as a female, makes conversation with the
child, and convinces him to send by phone a picture or his genitals. If the
child is a female, the adult simply pretends to be a young child close to the
victim's age.

Once the adult has the picture, he reveals himself and uses it to
blackmail the child, threatening to expose the picture to parents or post it
on the Web if the child does not do what he wants. It is likely that what
he is going to want in exchange is some type of sexual act from the child.
This type of blackmail could go on for a long time, as the child will be
afraid the picture will be shown to parents, relatives, or friends. This is a
crime that is severely underreported, because all too often, the victim will
not report it to anyone, for fear of embarrassment.

The following is another underreported but all-too-common occurrence.
Names, of course, are withheld for obvious reasons.

CASE STUDY

A ten-year-old girl who lives with her mother in the suburbs of a large city
ponders how life will be now that her mother has recently remarried. Her
mother's new husband has always been nice to her, but she has reason to be
distrustful, and deep down she wishes her mother wouldn't be as trusting
all the time. Since she was seven, her mother has always left her at the
homes of family members while she worked, ran errands, or went out on
the town on dates. This seemed to work out at first, but after a while, it
turned into a nightmare, because the aunt her mother left her with from

time to time had a son who had just turned seventeen. At night, this cousin would come into her room and rape her every time she stayed. She was afraid to tell anyone for a long time and did not feel like she could talk to her mother.

Now that her mother was married, she was already noticing that her stepdad was staring at her and looking in on her at night when he thought she was sleeping. Time went on, and the marriage between the girl's mother and stepfather began to get rocky. The mother started going out late at night staying out until 4:00 in the morning, sometimes leaving the girl and her brother home. The stepfather's frustrations began to build. He would argue with the girl's mother every time it happened. He suspected she was being unfaithful, but he had no proof.

The stepfather was angered by this more and more each time. One night when the mother left, the stepfather came into the girl's room and raped her. This would go on for the next five years, every time the mother would go out late at night and not come home. The girl never told her mother or anyone else. Her mother remained married to the stepfather without knowing what he had done. They somehow strangely co-existed, with the mother having no idea and the stepfather pretending it never happened and the young girl—now an adult with a daughter of her own—living in torment, thinking over and over again of what happened. The girl's own daughter came to know the stepfather as her grandfather but would always wonder why her mother would never allow her to stay at home alone with her own grandfather.

*   *   *

This is a story that is as true as it is unfortunate and all too common. The story illustrates how easily and secretly these issues can occur within a family setting and not come to light, especially when your child feels he or she cannot talk to you. To the untrained eye, it appears that the father became angry with the actions of the mother and wanted to hurt her in the same way she was hurting him with her suspected infidelity. The truth is, the person the stepfather really hurt was the child, who now has to live an entire life with what he has done. This little girl was victimized not by one person but by at least two and didn't feel that she could tell someone.

The true tragedy is when something happens and the child doesn't feel he or she can tell someone. At that point, the issue remains in the dark and never comes to light. The criminal act goes unpunished, and the victim never gets any assistance.

Always remember that this type of mental trauma is too much for someone to deal with alone, especially a child. Chances are, if the child has to deal with this alone, other problems will manifest themselves as a result.

COMMUNICATE WITH YOUR CHILD

The different aspects of personal safety can be a complicated issue. They involve trends, behavior, and what to recognize as inconsistencies in others. A parent may find it challenging to break down to a child in the simplest terms how to be safe. The child's age, maturity level, and ability to comprehend will dictate how much information you can convey to your child or children. You the parent or guardian are still the best person to teach the child about personal safety.

The most important thing you can communicate to your children is that they can tell you or talk to you about anything. This point must be consistently driven home in the child's mind, daily if necessary. A pedophile's best tool is to foster secrecy between parent and child. The pedophile knows that is his best chance of going undetected. You simply have to go on the offensive and beat any potential offender to the punch by telling your child that in every situation, it is okay to tell a parent or guardian something. Do this by simply going over every possible scenario with your child. And for each, tell the child it is okay to talk to you, that it is not the child's fault, and you are not going to be angry with the child about any information relayed. Go over with your child some of the following scenarios.

Scenario/possible manipulations an offender may say to a child	Your possible response to child
I will give you all the candy you want to eat, but you cannot tell your parents or they would put an end to it.	I won't be mad about any candy or gift you already took. This person is trying to trick you with these things, and I need to know.
You can come over and play all my video games, but don't tell your mom that you are over here every day.	There are people out there who may want to hurt you, even though they seem friendly. I need to know where you are.
If you tell your parents what has been going on, I will have to hurt them.	I can protect myself better if you tell me that a threat has been made. This person is trying to scare you, and probably won't hurt anyone.
If you tell, you will be in trouble, just like me.	It is never your fault when an adult harms you. It is always the fault of the adult.
This is our little secret, so you can't tell anyone.	If someone tells you not to tell your parents something, they're probably up to no good. You can talk to me about anything.
Your parents would not understand, so you can't tell them.	The person telling you this knows I will understand what is happening. What he's telling you isn't true, and it's dangerous.
You don't have to tell your parents your every move; they don't need to know everything you do.	I'm responsible for making sure you are safe. To do that, I need to know what you are doing.
If you are a scaredy-cat, I understand.	You don't have to prove anything to anyone! If something makes you feel uncomfortable, then don't do it.

These are just some of the tactics and statements that a sex offender might use to verbally coerce a child. In the examples used, the responses are only generalized. You should tailor your responses to fit the situation, age, and comprehension of the child. What is important in your response is that you communicate to the child that you won't be angry with him or her and it is okay to inform you what is happening. You have to build a foundation that will show your child that you won't overreact to disturbing information. This simply means that you should give the child proper credit for general honesty as often as you can.

Generally, when the child informs you of something he or she did wrong, you should acknowledge his or her honesty and willingness to come forth unprompted, even if you have to punish the child for the improper conduct you learned of. This should be done as calmly as the situation will allow. Over time, the child will note how he or she is disciplined; the fairer the child perceives your treatment to be, the more he or she may feel comfortable disclosing information, even when they feel they have done something wrong.

In addition to the importance of your child communicating information to you, it is just as important to continue to communicate with your child, even if it doesn't seem to be effective. Often, repetition has to be used in communicating ideas to adults, because they sometimes do not actively listen. The same is true with children. Set boundaries with your children about where they may go, things they may do, and people they are allowed to see.

POINTS TO PONDER THUS FAR

- A parent should know who the children's friends are and what adults they talk to.

- A parent should know where their children are at all times.

- A parent should tell the child to notify them if the child is going somewhere and plans change.

- Parents should reinforce their openness and willingness to have the child talk to them about *any* matter, good or bad.

Up until this point, the suggested communication between parent and child has been generalized in relation to subject matter that should be conveyed. Keep in mind that it is very important for your child to understand every aspect of the danger posed by pedophiles and other offenders. You should not over-advise in such a way that would scare the child, but you should fully inform the child. For that reason, it is necessary to give further, more specific examples of ways to communicate to your child the dangers associated with pedophilia and other abuse. As always, tailor what is given here in such a way that it will best suit your style of dialogue with your child. It's important to communicate the true meaning of a message, more so than how you say it.

CHAPTER 2

WHAT CHILD AND PARENT CAN DO

There are a few things your child should know and be able to repeat if needed. Again the child's age and ability to comprehend will dictate how much of the following the child will absorb, but the more the better.

Knowing as many of the following as possible will greatly assist your child if there is an emergency. Try to teach them as many as you can.

- Child's full name
- Home number or cell phone of parent
- Home number or cell phone number of other trusted adult
- Home address
- Parents' work address or name of business
- Parents' full name(s)

As with any list you find written in this book, it is never exhaustive of everything you can teach or look out for. Feel free to add or take away from it, to suit your individual need.

Included on the list of things your child can use in an emergency should be the utilization of a **safe site**. A safe site is an area or place in your town you could designate as a meeting place, should you and your child ever be separated for any reason. If your child is ever abducted, there is a possibility that he or she may be able to escape the abductor at some point.

If the child has no real plan after that, it may be easier for the abductor to relocate him or her. For this reason, you may want to designate some safe sites that your child could utilize in this situation. Go over these sites with your child and tell the child that these are the first areas you would check if he or she was ever lost or abducted.

This may be difficult to do if you live in a very large city. In that case, you should tell your child to go to the nearest public facility in the area, such as a fire station, bank, park, or, of course, a police station. As stated previously, this will work a lot better in a smaller community, where you can designate a specific place. Once you designate a specific place, you can tell your child you will check the designated area daily for as long as he or she is missing. It would be a good idea to designate a safe site on each end of town, not just the area you reside in.

It is not recommended that you depend on a safe site designation with your child as a *primary* plan of action, but as a thoughtful secondary tool, especially if your child has not memorized your home number or cell phone number. Children who have memorized their parents' numbers could simply go to anyplace near where they are lost to call. Safe-site designations are better suited for children who would not be able to call their parents or make contact with another responsible adult.

Talking to Your Child Specifically of Sexual Abuse

Much of what we have discussed already is generalized in relation to communication with your child. It is important, however, that they understand what sexual abuse is and when it may be happening to them. There are certain key things you will need to communicate to your child, and the following discussion is only a guideline. Select your wording according to the child's age and comprehension level, and sometimes gender may be of consideration.

The discussion with your child about sexual abuse should be as open as you can possibly make it. More than likely, the child will have some general questions about sexual development and behavior. You should answer these as best you can based on the child's age and comprehension level. The areas of discussion to follow have been broken down in phases; however, you can re-arrange them in any way you like.

PHASE 1

When speaking of the sexual organs, try to use the proper names for each. However, with younger children, phrases like *private parts* or *private areas* may be more appropriate. You should tell your child to inform you immediately if anyone touches them there or exposes those areas to them. This should also include anyone who might try to take pictures of their private areas or even talk to them about these areas or about sex in general. Expand this conversation to include anything that would make them feel uncomfortable. Let them know that if they don't feel right about something, they should tell you. There is a good chance during this phase of conversation that the child will ask you what sex is or have questions about it. Again tailor your answer to what you deem appropriate to their age and level of comprehension.

PHASE 2

Tell your child that some adults have issues that cause them to want to touch children in these areas. Expand that to explain that some of these troubled adults have sex with children, in addition to other acts of abuse.

Tell your child that problems like these in adults are wrong, in the same way stealing or hitting would be. Advise them that just like stealing and hitting, sexual abuse is also wrong. Tell them that it is important that they inform you of any adult with this problem, so the problem can be dealt with appropriately. Do not categorize sexual abuse as a sickness; this may result in unhelpful sympathy from the child for an offender. Remind them that some offenders try to trick children into keeping abuse a secret. Tell them that is only for the offender's benefit and that secrets like those are not to be kept from you. Give them some examples of things an offender may say to get children to remain silent about this crime. We covered this in the last chapter but you may be able to think of more examples to go over.

PHASE 3

Explain to your child that it is not okay to touch another person's private parts and that they should not engage in any touching of another's private area. Reiterate that you will not be mad at them if they tell you they have engaged in this activity, even if it has been going on for a while. Explain to them that sexual abuse is a crime, and every crime has a victim and a suspect, and sometimes witnesses. Tell them that the victim is never to blame for a criminal act.

Talk to your children on safety issues often; give them "what-if" scenarios, and see how they answer. Have them pick out at least two other responsible adults whom you trust your child could talk to if they felt they couldn't talk to you. Make the phone numbers of those adults readily available to them.

WHAT YOUR CHILD CAN DO

This section will discuss some ideas of things parents as well as children can do to make themselves safer against individuals who would harm them if given the opportunity. There are often little things parents and children generally don't think of that may make a world of difference if your child is ever targeted by an offender. As with anything else, adopting some or all the following ideas may be of some use. As a parent or guardian of our most precious resource, you can decide.

SAFETY AT HOME AND IN THE NEIGHBORHOOD

- Get out and meet your neighbors. Know who they are.
- Check your local sex offender registry to find out what sex offenders may be living near you.
- Tell your children whose home, if any, they are allowed to visit.
- Set up boundaries in your community that your children are not permitted to cross.
- Advise your children never to let anyone know if they are home alone.
- Have emergency phone numbers beside the phone in your home.

SCHOOL SAFETY

- If you must put your child's name on the outside of their backpack, use first initial and last name. Ideally you may want to write the child's name on the inside of their things. (Listing first names can put an abductor on a first-name basis with your child.)
- Walk the route to the school or bus stop area if possible.
- Tell your child to tell you of anyone in or out of the school system who makes them feel uncomfortable (even if it's the principal or a teacher).

- Know who your child's school friends are and the parents of those friends if possible.

WHAT YOUR CHILD CAN DO (younger children)

- Know their full name.
- Know their address.
- Know their parents' name(s).
- Check with a parent before accepting anything from anyone.
- Check with a parent before going anywhere with anyone.
- Take a friend when they go places or to play outside.
- Say no to anything that makes them feel uncomfortable.
- Tell a parent or trusted adult if someone tries to touch them or does anything else that makes them feel uncomfortable.

Empower your children. Let them know that they are important and they have the right to be secure. Sex offenders often prey on children who have a low self-image. They use that information to manipulate the child in several different ways. The best way to combat this is to let your children know that they are loved and they are very important to you.

WHAT YOUR CHILD CAN DO (older children)

- Avoid going out alone.
- Know parents' home and cell numbers.
- Know safe sites and boundaries established by parents.
- Say no if they are feeling threatened.
- Don't engage in idle conversation with strangers.
- Don't accept any gifts from strangers.
- Notify parent of anything that makes them feel uncomfortable.
- Never accept a ride from a stranger or adult your parents have not authorized you to ride with.
- If going home alone after school, call parents when they arrive, to let them know they are okay.
- If home alone, don't advise people who call the residence of this.

Parents of older children may want to seriously consider providing their child with a cell phone. Some parents have strong feelings about giving their children cell phones, and understandably so. However, cell phones can be purchased that can only dial certain numbers, as well as cell phones that can be tracked with GPS. It is definitely something to consider.

Different ways you can use technological developments to protect your child will be explored later in the book.

One can never use too many precautionary methods when it comes to the safety of a child. The more one can think of, the better. Some additional methods will be provided later in this book. You can use them to document some things about your child that may be useful if you have to mass produce and share information in a hurry.

It is a good idea to compile the following data about your child:

- A complete description of your child.
- Medical information or where records can be located.
- Dental charts.
- A sample of your child's DNA.
- Copies of your child fingerprints.
- Color photo of the child (update every six months; video is also good).
- Items that your child has worn or handled excessively.

The last item on the list was added because scent-tracking dogs are often used if a child is missing and it is believed he or she can be located nearby. No doubt there will be plenty of objects around the house that will have the child's scent on them. However, you might want to retain an item your child has worn and seal it in a plastic bag. This should ensure quick and easy access when you need it fast, as well as the most robust of scents for the dog.

GATHERING THE FACTS— NUTS AND BOLTS (Child History And Prints)

In this section, you will find some forms you can use to gather information on your child. As with anything else in this book, you may want to gather more or less information; use your best judgment. If you fill in these forms with your child's information, you should tear those pages from this book, unless you intend to secure the entire book in a safe place.

Gathering all the facts is the most important thing you can do in the protection of your child. In a crisis, it may be too late to gather this pertinent information quickly. You want to have all the information on your child in a centralized location, so you can hand it directly to the police. In some cases, you may need to make many copies of the information as well. Either way, it is helpful to have everything necessary in a centralized location.

The following are information-collecting forms you can use. In many cities, local police have child safety programs. If so, program officers can fingerprint and document certain facts about your child. If your city does not have such a program, the following forms may prove useful.

Personal Data on Child

> **Your child's
> photo here.
> Update every
> six months.**

Date of Photo: _____

Date of Birth: _____

Full Name: _____

Nickname: _____

Race: _____

Height: _____   Weight _____

Build _____

Eye color _____   Hair color _____

Complexion _____

SSN: _____

Distinguishing marks _____

_____

Medical Conditions _____

_____

Blood type: _____

Place of birth (*city, state, hospital*) _____

_____

Doctor's name: _____

Doctor's address and phone number: _____

_____

Dentist Name: _____

Dentist Address and Phone Number _____

_____

TAPE CHILD'S DNA SAMPLE HERE

A piece of hair pulled from the root may work best here.

Child's fingerprint record—right hand

Right thumb	Right Index	Right Middle

Right Ring	Right Little	Right four fingers

Child's fingerprint record—left hand

Left thumb	Left Index	Left Middle
Left Ring	Left Little	Left four fingers

NOTES:

POLICE CONTACT FORM

(Can be used to make personal notes of an incident.)

Date of incident _____

Date of call to police _____

First responder officer name _____

Detective assigned _____

Case number _____

Was an entry made into NCIC? _____

Description of what child was wearing _____

_____

_____

CHAPTER 3

THE EMERGENCY
(Steps To Take When Crisis Occurs)

It is a sad reality that thousands of children in this country each year are abused in some way. Sexual as well as other types of abuse usually have adverse affects on children, to the extent that professional help is often needed. The end result in many cases is that the abused will one day become an abuser. This is not always true, but often abuse creates a kind of cycle that if not broken will continue from one person to the next. Some victims of abuse never go on to abuse anyone, however one thing about sexual abuse is an unfortunate truth: if your child is sexually abused, there is no doubt it will change that child's life forever.

But if you can be there for your child and know how to respond properly, you can help your child to work through it. The sincere hope is that abuse will never happen, but if it does, someone has to be there so the child can adjust to life after abuse.

This chapter will focus on dealing with a crisis in two areas: if your child is missing and if your child is actually sexually abused. The chapter will fashion a template for a proper response to each. As with all other chapters in this book, adjust your responses to your needs and those of the child.

Since a missing child requires the most immediate action, we will start there. If your child is ever abducted or lost, the sooner you can discover the occurrence, the better chance you have of recovery. This is one reason why you should know where your child is at all times. If you know your child's whereabouts and daily routine to the letter, you will know very quickly when your child is missing.

The first thing you will have to do once you confirm there is a problem is immediately call your local law-enforcement agency. Your local police department will have primary jurisdiction in the beginning. Do not attempt to call another jurisdiction or agency first; this will only waste time, as they will only refer you to the primary agency. For example, if you live in Little Rock, Arkansas, and your child is abducted, the Little Rock Police Department will have primary jurisdiction. Whether other agencies get involved depends heavily on the circumstances. If there is evidence that the child was abducted and taken across state lines, the FBI may become involved. The quality of the preliminary investigation may be only as good as the local agency that conducts it. Ideas on ways to rate your local agency will be discussed later in the book.

If your child is abducted, the second thing that needs to be done after the police are called is to enter the child into the National Crime Information Center (NCIC) Missing Persons File. In order to accomplish this, you will have to provide the police with certain pertinent information about your child for entry into the file. If you filled out the child personal history data in chapter 2 of this book, you can simply hand the officer the pages. At the same time, law enforcement should be canvassing the immediate area with all other available units. The primary officer there with you should gather a description of your child and put out a radio broadcast to these units.

In the meantime, only allow law enforcement initial and full access to your home. No doubt concerned relatives will be coming by to offer support. Limit these individuals to one room until the police tell you it is clear. The police may want to collect evidence from the home, more specifically the child's room. Probably the most vital information you can relay to law enforcement is the time you last saw your child and what your child was wearing when you last saw them. It is vital to give the police your full cooperation; the slightest detail you remember, even one you think is insignificant, may make a world of difference in the case.

If your child meets the criteria, an Amber Alert or similar warning system can be utilized to further get the word of your missing child out to the public. For the most part, you will have to rely heavily on law enforcement to investigate the matter, but that doesn't mean there's nothing more you can do. The following are a few ideas.

- Make flyers including photo, age, height, and weight of the child, what they were wearing last, and a phone number to call with information.

- Organize family and friends and conduct a search of unsearched areas. Have these individuals pass out the flyers as well.

- If the media is not already aware, contact them to see if they can do a story.

- Contact the police, and get the name and number of the detective assigned to your case. Provide this individual with any new information.

- Be polite but persistent in all you do.

You may be able to think of even more things that you can do. Getting on the Internet via e-mail and chat rooms, even a Web page dedicated to your abducted child are also valuable resources. Through the Internet, you can get the word out to vast numbers of people. The best advice would be to contact someone who has expertise in Web design about designing a page dedicated to the issues involving your child. In many cases, you may be able to find an individual willing to donate their time. There really are no bad ideas; the more you can think of, the better. The unfortunate truism to missing children is, the child may be recovered quickly within hours or days, or the child may go on missing for years. If the latter is true, it will no doubt result in days filled with an agony that never seems to end. You should never give up. There have been children located alive who had been missing for years. The truth is, you never know, so you have to continue to try.

The next thing to be discussed is what to do if your child is actually abused but not abducted. This is an especially sensitive subject, as there are many areas of concern. If this should ever happen to your child, there is a good chance that the child will never be the same again. The event is sure to change the child forever in some way or another. The best you as the parent can hope to do is minimize the effects of the abuse. This means providing emotional support as well as any psychological support that your child may need from a professional.

There is always a danger that if left untreated, a victim of abuse may go on to victimize others. While some studies are still inconclusive, many abusers do suggest that they were abused in childhood themselves. Since these statements often come at the time they are caught, it can sometimes be hard to tell how much is accurate and how much is the exercise of excuse.

If your child is ever abused, there are a few basic things you will need to do for the benefit of your child. The most basic of things to remember is to take care of your child first. Everything else will have to come second, at least temporarily. There will be ample time to deal with other matters later.

From the moment your child tells you that they have been the victim of abuse, whether it be full sexual abuse or inappropriate touching, the first thing you have to do is stay calm. You want the child to divulge all the information to you and feel as comfortable as possible doing so. An adverse reaction of any kind by you may cause the child to feel afraid, ashamed, or guilty, thus making it harder for them to talk about the incident.

Therefore, rule number one is:

1. BE QUIET AND LISTEN!

When the child first indicates that they want to discuss an incident of this nature, you should start by reassuring them that it is okay to tell you and that you are not going to be angry with them. Also tell the child that you are going to take care of things and that you are glad they came to you about the issue. But be brief; it's time for the child to talk. It may even be better to reserve all comments previously mentioned until the end in some cases. It may be best to keep it simple at first: "Tell me what happened," or something to that effect should be one of the last things you say. Then it's time to be quiet and listen. Let the child relay the events, and try not to interrupt unless you absolutely have to. Do not interrupt the initial story for times and dates; you can always ask about these details when the child has finished talking. Just like with adults, if you interrupt the child in mid-sentence, something the child may intend to say could be lost, so try not to do it.

After you have gathered all the facts, you should report the incident to authorities without any further delay. The local law-enforcement agency should be your first contact. Other organizations like the Child Abuse Hotline should come second. Remember, there is always a chance that the abuser could be abusing more than just your child, so by reporting it promptly, you are not only helping your child, but you may be helping someone else's child.

Do not, under any circumstances, take matters into your own hands by confronting the abuser yourself in any way. From this point on, you want to help create a solid legal case against the abuser. Any adverse action you take could be counterproductive. Remember, your child needs you to be available and there for them; let the police handle the offender.

Next tell your child you would like them to tell the authorities everything they just told you and that it is okay to do so. Tell the child that from that point on, he or she must have no further contact with the offender. Assure the child that what happened is not their fault. Try not to put a lot of emphasis on the fact that the offender will be in trouble, because you don't want to make the child feel guilty. This could hinder the flow of information from your child to you. But do tell the child that the blame for what happened rests with the offender.

In any case, there is nothing better than a live eyewitness to a crime, versus third- and fourth-hand information. Your goal and your role are to facilitate the free flow of information. Initially your child should only have to repeat the story twice: first to you and then to the police. The criminal justice system may require them to recount it a few more times as well. That may be what it takes to get a conviction of the offender. What should be avoided are notifications to different family members and friends who may arrive before the police. Try to fight the temptation to alert other family members of the crime when your child initially tells you of abuse.

That way, you avoid having anything tainted by comments of others. It will be difficult, but wait until after the police have responded before calling anyone else. If the case goes to trial, a defense attorney will use anything he can to diminish your child's testimony. Don't facilitate the option for the defense; preserve your child's testimony.

In all of this, don't forget about yourself. If you have been strong enough to get through it without showing the raw emotion that is inherent in such an event, you will likely need some assistance yourself. Seek support for yourself in whatever way you can. You may find you need someone to talk to about the situation, or you may need more professional help in coping. In any event, do not discuss the incident with your support person in front of the child. The probability of any emotional healing of your child will depend greatly on your actions and how you handle the issue. Many experts believe that parent and child must seek professional help in the form of a psychologist or other professional.

It cannot be stressed enough how difficult it will be for your child, should they ever be abducted, abused, or both. In most cases, such an event will change your child completely from the child they were. It is recommended that a parent utilize whatever assistance that is offered, if it will benefit the child in these instances.

PEDOPHILES—
WHO AND WHAT THEY ARE

Merriam-Webster (2010) defines pedophilia as "sexual perversions in which children are the preferred sexual object or a preferential or exclusive sexual attraction by adults to prepubescent youths." *The Child/Adult Safety Bible* will go a step further in expanding on defining pedophilia. Pedophilia is the misguided sexual attraction by an adult to a prepubescent youth, which has a root in a perverted and compartmentalized evil, as it may be the one evil component in a individuals behavior. When this attraction is acted upon, it is illegal in the United States. For an individual to be merely attracted to prepubescent youths may indicate a problem but is not a crime. For this reason, it is very difficult to gauge how many individuals are actually dangerous to children before they act. A pedophile is simply someone who has an attraction to prepubescent children; they become offenders when they act on their impulses.

Most would agree, at a minimum, the practice of pedophilia is immoral, and the fact of the matter is that acting on it is illegal. The mystery of pedophilia is how a person can seem well-rounded on the outside and appear relatively normal but have thoughts of improper relationships with young children. Evil can be a *part* of someone, meaning the whole of the individual's actions may not be evil. This is why a person who is a danger to a child is so hard to detect; the evil is specific and compartmentalized within the individual.

In the Holy Bible, there is a passage in Proverbs 28:1 that reads, "The wicked flee when no man pursueth, but the righteous are bold as a lion." The wicked flee because in their mind, they know what they have done before anyone else finds out about it. So in light of that, they will also begin to cover their tracks before they are detected. The same is true with pedophiles and individuals who actually offend. They know what they are long before you do, and this can put the victim at a disadvantage.

A soldier who had just come home from the war in Iraq once said,

"The hardest thing about fighting the enemy over there was the fact that it was like fighting an unseen enemy. A person who you think is a merchant or non-combatant may come out from around a corner and take a shot at you, then go back to selling goods on the sidewalk. After a while, it's hard to identify who the enemy is." In a sense, the same is true in combating sex offenders and pedophiles, specifically because often you can't see the thoughts birthed in their heads until they act on them. Unfortunately, by the time they do, it is often too late, as by then, at least one child has been abused.

Pedophiles occupy every social and economic level of our society. Like a virus, it may not be readily and immediately visible who is affected. As stated earlier, many have urges but never act on them, but like a time bomb, you don't know when they will, either. This type of pedophile may maintain and view child pornography in secret and may build an entire collection without the knowledge of the live-in spouse or others around them.

Often, the older a pedophile is, the more extensive the collection of child pornography. Pedophiles do not limit themselves merely to child pornography; they often collect child erotica, which may include photos, drawings, and cutouts from newspapers and magazines depicting children. The short video clip of JonBenet Ramsey participating in a Colorado beauty pageant is said to have found its way into the video libraries of pedophiles across the country. Unlike erotica, the mere possession of child pornography is a crime, and any adult known to be in possession of it should always be reported to the police.

These **dormant pedophiles** may go years and never offend, or they may never offend in their lives, but the potential for danger is always there. If these types of pedophiles offend, it will almost always be an offense of convenience that will involve a child they have unlimited or easy access to. These potential offenders are almost impossible to identify. If they can hide their carnal desires for children from their spouse, they can most certainly hide it from a parent or potential victim. These are a little more dangerous than the offender who is widely known or registered. Curled back in hiding like a rattlesnake, they simply patiently wait for the most opportune time to strike.

The only advice and guard that can be given against an offender of this type who has yet to offend is, pay attention to any potential signs and go with your gut. If you get bad feelings about an individual, don't leave your child alone with them or in their care. Better to offend someone slightly than to be too polite and entrust your child to someone you don't feel comfortable with. Most responsible adults will understand a parent's concern for their child. If they don't, that is unfortunate, but never waiver or allow someone to cause you to dismiss your concerns.

Some experts tend to break pedophilia down further, but in practical terms, there are really only three types of sex offenders: those who are actively offending, those who have offended in the past, and those who lay dormant and collect erotica and child porn, waiting for the right opportunity to offend.

Pedophiles generally use erotica and child porn in four ways: self-gratification, introduction to the child, to blackmail the child, and for profit by selling and trading material with other pedophiles and active offenders. There is an underground demand for child pornography that fuels desire of some to obtain these materials. A pedophile/offender may use child pornography to introduce the idea of sex to an unsuspecting child; this also serves to downplay the seriousness of the act and lower the inhibitions of the child and may be one of the first seduction methods to sexual abuse an offender may try.

As mentioned previously, the offender may also create his own child pornography by taking photos of a child in compromising positions, in order to use them as blackmail against the child. This may be very effective if the parent has never discussed the scenario with the child and assured them that they should report anything that makes them feel uncomfortable.

Pedophiles and offenders tend to place high value on their individual erotica and pornography collections. There have been documented cases where sex offenders asked to have seized pornography given back to them after they were released from jail.

Police booking Photo of Chester Stiles

A good example of a dangerous pedophile involving child pornography would be a case in Las Vegas, Nevada, where police obtained a video from a third party of a possible three-year-old girl being sexually assaulted by an adult male. Police at the time believed the suspect to be Chester Stiles. Police didn't go into detail about the assault, but it was said to be horrific. Investigators were able to determine that the tape was roughly three to four years old in September of 2007, when it was obtained. A search for the victim found a seven-year-old girl who was safe and sound with family and apparently had no recollection of the attack.

Initially, the individual who first turned the tape in to police was arrested on possession of child pornography and other charges. It was unclear how long he possessed the tape before turning it in. It is likely the police suspected the tape had been in circulation for a time after it was made. Stiles was later convicted of the crime.

Again, this is typical, for child pornography to be passed around in this manner for years. This material has a high value among pedophiles. One can only guess how much money changes hands in the trade of such material. In turn, the victims depicted in the material are victimized over and over again, even into adulthood. Individuals who collect this material create a demand in which the law has to be broken to satisfy.

An individual may try to make an argument that there was no harm in the mere collection of this material, but that is not true. The demand itself will cause another individual to then break the law by exploiting a child somewhere to obtain photos and video images. Each individual involved is equally responsible and guilty for his own actions, but it does create a chain reaction or domino effect. The end result is the child victim at the end of the chain with nothing to gain in the matter and almost everything to lose.

When you consider the chain reaction of it all and look even further down the chain, you will find that a large percentage of abusers were abused themselves in their childhood. It doesn't take much additional research at all to see that this theoretical chain forms a circle, and the abuse continues if the circle is not broken.

The good news is, you as a parent can arm yourself with knowledge and break the chain with your child and in your community when you see abuse occurring.

CHAPTER 4

YOUR LOCAL POLICE—
THE QUALITY OF THE FORCE

B ecause your local police will probably have primary jurisdiction should your child ever be a victim of a crime, it is important to discuss the framework, at least in general, of first responders. The majority of people have little control over where they live and what agency's jurisdiction they fall under. The better a parent can understand what kind of law-enforcement agency they are dealing with before they need them, the more they will understand what is happening at a given point when they do.

Many people believe as a general rule that all law-enforcement agencies and personnel are the same. Some believe if you report something to one officer or agency, you have covered all the reporting and notifying that needs to be done. It is crucial to know that this is not the case; as a matter of fact, it's not even close to being true.

Different law-enforcement agencies have different primary responsibilities, jurisdictions, and most importantly, different levels of training. Some officers receive better, and more specified training than others, which varies based on a variety of factors. This is not to say that an officer with little or unspecified training is not just as dedicated or serious about his job as a well-trained officer, but the tools afforded an officer may be different.

Depending on the situation, it may not even be an issue of training.

For example, you wouldn't ask an FBI agent to assist you in investigating a traffic accident; that is not what the FBI does, so their ability to assist a citizen with that is going to be very limited. The best thing to do is not simply look at the badge and gun but read the badge and actually take into account what that particular law-enforcement person specializes in. This will save a lot of grief and misunderstanding down the road.

Most professionals are hesitant to make any distinction, in order to avoid stepping on any toes or ruffling the feathers of any individuals to whom their words might apply, but the fact is that some agencies simply perform better than others. A local agency may be more effective than a federal or state law-enforcement agency or vice versa. How good an agency is at what it is tasked to do will depend on a lot of very complicated factors. Funding, training, leadership, and experience doing what it is tasked to do are among the most important factors. For example, a New York Police homicide detective may perform better than any state or federal investigator in the area of investigating homicides, due to the sheer experience advantage he or she may have in investigating more of these types of crimes.

There are a lot of twist and turns to the complexity of rating the effectiveness of a police agency, because generally they perform a wide variety of law enforcement and sometimes administrative tasks. Another example of experience in performing required tasks would be a small town with a population of two thousand and a police department of five officers suddenly tasked to handle a homicide investigation, when there hasn't been a homicide in the town in seven years. The department could be well-funded and well-trained, but the lack of experience in investigating a homicide would affect the investigation.

The more well-rounded a department in funding, experience, and leadership, the better the department will be and the better it will serve the public. Leadership is so important to the success of a department or agency that it can overcome other shortcomings. Good, solid leadership from the top down can make up for a lack of experience, funding, and sometimes training.

The reason that it can only sometimes make up for lack of good training is because the leader of an agency is rarely a first responder. A good leader comes along and makes good decisions shortly after the fact. So if the first responder is not properly trained, things may already be in a downward spiral before the leader can get a footing on what has occurred.

How all this might affect you, for the purposes of the topics in this book, is the police's ability to investigate, prevent, or protect your child in an incident where he or she may be the victim of a crime at the hand of a child predator or pedophile.

Most of what you need to know can be found in public records as it relates to the performance of an agency. Most police departments track and record their own record of average response time. If they do, this is usually a matter of public record and can tell you a lot about a department. An average response time of five minutes or less for first responders is excellent but rare; ten minutes is more common. Anything over that is not very good. If you have any doubt, simply imagine yourself calling the police to report your child missing or some other critical incident and having to wait fifteen minutes or more for the police to arrive.

It should be noted that response time depends on a number of factors. Time of day the call was received, number of calls holding, and the position of the unit that received the call will all come into play.

Just like any other profession, police have peak hours of the day when they are busier than other times. When this happens, more calls for service may come in than there are police units to handle them. These calls have to be placed in a hold status for the next available unit. This is usually done by priority, with the most serious calls being dispatched first. Additionally, this will generally cause a domino effect, because the next available unit may be further away from the location that needs service. All these factors and more—some of which are beyond anyone's control—have an effect on response times.

Another statistic that can sometimes be checked is an agency's case closure rate or percentage. What type, and how many cases do they solve and at what rate? An agency's effectiveness when it comes to closing case investigations may be vital to how effectively they will handle your case, should you ever have one. Hopefully, you never will, but at any rate, it is good information, as it is always good to know the effectiveness of the agency you are working with.

The credentials of the lead detectives, division captains, and even the chief himself should be accessible, if need be. Most of the time an agency is only as good as its leadership. This brings up another point: inquire into how an agency promotes its personnel, mainly its detectives. Most require a test and an assessment center be completed; however, the author of this book once worked at an agency where a time-in-service requirement, a biographical-skills sheet and panel interview (but no test) were the only obstacles that had to be overcome to make detective. At the end of the day, this was little more than a popularity contest, in the author's opinion. If your child is ever a victim of a crime, do you want the most popular detective or the smartest on your case? This may not be relevant to the agency in your area but it may be good to know how these things are handled in your local agency.

Lastly, good old word of mouth is still the best way to gather information on the quality of an individual or an agency's work. Ask law-abiding citizens in the community what they think about the agency and its history in servicing the community. If there is a negative that is a constant, it will become apparent very quickly.

To sum it all up in a few sentences: from locality to locality, all police departments are different, with different policies and procedures. What one will do or can do, another may not. Most of the time, there is no uniformity in their training from state to state; some are trained very well and are very advanced in what they learn, while some may just receive basic or general law-enforcement training. Each local police agency may run its own academy or contract with a state-run academy. Some basic state standards may be the same, but some training will vary from academy to academy. Make no mistake: the dedication level runs pretty deep, and that, along with good leadership and motivation, can make up for what an agency may lack in training.

Nothing said here is meant to put down or disparage any one particular agency, but the public has a right and need to know that not every agency is the same in how they handle an incident and how effective they are. Finally, police often keep statistics on crime rates in certain areas, for example how many burglaries or robberies may occur in a certain neighborhood. If they do, this is public information, and every citizen has a right to it. If you are considering moving to a certain area or just want to know the statistics in the area where you already live, it is a good idea to request this information.

CHAPTER 5

PERSONAL SECURITY

This chapter deals with individual and personal security. When the phrase "personal security and safety" is invoked, one usually thinks of women and children, but personal safety applies to everyone. Anyone can be a victim of violent crime—young, old, male, female, rich, poor.

Personal security breaks down into many categories of when and where it should be practiced. These categories may include but are not limited to home and family security, computer and telephone security, as well as travel and identity security, to name a few. Some simple everyday tips, as we will discuss here, will go a long way when it comes to covering the bases on personal security.

One of the most precious and important things you will ever secure, besides yourself, is your home and family. Some methods of security are common-sense, while others may be more technical. Either way, there is no bad advice, only applicable and inapplicable.

HOME AND FAMILY

ACCESS

- Always restrict the accessibility to your home. This means keeping all doors and windows closed and locked when you are not home.

Limit the number of keys to your home you give out. Change the locks every time if keys are lost.

- Lock all entrances to the home, even when you are there. Home-intrusion crimes are on the rise. The fact that the home is occupied is not a deterrent for some criminals. If an individual wants access to your home that badly, it's unlikely any door ever made could truly stop him, but the time it may take a criminal to negotiate the obstacle of a locked door may buy you time to call the police, trigger the alarm, or take defensive action.

- Get to know your neighbors and the cars that belong to people who live in the area. This makes it easier to recognize when something is out of place. In turn, your neighbor being a little familiar with your practices will help him or her be more aware when things are out of place at your home as well.

- If necessary, contact your local police department to request extra patrols in your area. Many agencies will have a unit ride through an area twice as often as they normally do if you request it. Some also perform this service if you are out of town on vacation.

SECURITY

- Shred and destroy all envelopes and statements that display your name, address, and account number when you are done using them. Ideally, a shredder, which is relatively inexpensive, should be used. If you don't have one, simply rip the statement up with your hands.

- Arrange for an unlisted phone number so your address will not be as readily accessible. Contact Internet providers that provide online maps, and ask to opt out with any providers who provide a picture or a map to your house when the address is punched in. This is a topic that is currently under litigation, but regardless of the outcome, the option to opt out and request that your information not be provided has always been there.

- Refuse unordered packages, and check the credentials of any service providers from whom you didn't request service at your home.

- Do not put your last name on mailboxes or display outside the home.

- Talk with your family about the purchase of video surveillance cameras, a dog, guns, or Tasers to enhance security in your home. See which option your family is comfortable with, and make the choice that is best for you as a family.

- Instruct children to keep all doors and windows locked and never to admit strangers into the home. If home alone, never tell a phone caller or someone knocking at the door that you are indeed home alone.

- Always note any suspicious vehicles in the area; write down the tag number if you can.

- There are a number of websites that list pedophiles or convicted sex offenders in your area. Be familiar with how many sex offenders are within ten miles or so, and familiarize yourself with the nature of their offense, if that information is listed. Most states have individualized sex-offender websites that list local offenders.

- The National Sex Offender Public Website hosted by the US Department of Justice is *www.nsopw.gov.*

When you go to the site, this is what you will see. You can search registries of all fifty states through this site.

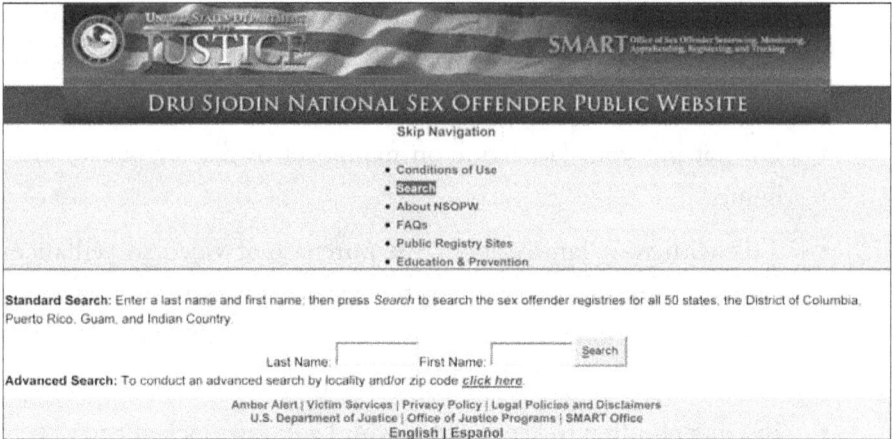

United States Department of Justice Dru Sjodin
National Sex Offender Public Website 2010.

TELEPHONE SAFETY

In some households, the phone rings often, with solicitors trying to sell something or obtain a donation to one cause or another, In most cases, it is as simple as that. In the worst of cases, it may be someone calling who would prey on your children or pull you into a scam if they have their way. The good news is, you don't have to let them have their way. Phone scams and phone predators are one of the few crimes you can control and possibly eliminate.

The thing to remember is that you are not obligated to speak with *anyone* who makes you feel uncomfortable on a phone you pay for. You have all kinds of power in this regard. The most powerful thing is to simply hang up. Technology exists that can redirect or block unwanted calls. You no longer have to pick the phone up to know who is calling.

It is a good rule of thumb to instruct children who are home alone not to answer the phone unless it is a parent or other adult whom you authorize to contact them when they are alone. With the use of a simple caller ID, it's easy to do. The best phones will have the caller ID built into them and a capacity to hold several numbers.

CASE STORY

A teen who came home every day after school and stayed alone in the home until her parents got off work would receive a daily phone call from a stranger. The teen thought this stranger was a representative of a child entertainment network. The stranger told the teen she had been awarded free membership in the network as a club member and was eligible to receive free comic books, gifts, and T-shirts.

The stranger, over the period of a few weeks, attempted to build a bond with the young girl. He nearly completed his mission, and before all was said and done, he knew the teen's address, where her parents worked, her parents' names, and when they got home every day. Thankfully, she happened to mention the calls to her parents before it was too late. The authorities were notified, only to find out it had been a convicted sex offender on the phone the whole time. Fortunately, he was found out before he had a chance to strike.

- Always instruct and advise your children how you want the phone in your home used.
- Instruct your children about what information they should and should not give out over the phone.
- Keep a list of emergency contact numbers near the phone at all times.
- Never speak about personal issues with a person over the phone whom you don't know.
- Report any suspicious phone calls to the proper authorities.

COMPUTER/ONLINE SAFETY AND SECURITY

Almost everyone is aware of the evils that have been perpetrated on our children and on many adults via the Internet. Computers and the Internet are very useful tools, but there are many individuals out there who use them as a mechanism to prey on the unsuspecting or the trusting.

The Internet is one of the main vehicles child predators use to prey on children. If your child is on the Internet, you should always monitor what sites and what chat rooms he or she visits. It is also possible to block your child from going to certain sites. There is technology available that makes this very easy to do.

Below are just a few basic rules of thumb regarding online safety with children and what you should instruct them to do.

- Never give out personal information online. (Define for your children what is considered personal, like home addresses, names, birthdates, parents' employment and so on.)
- Never agree to meet anyone in person whom they may have spoken with online.
- Report any solicitation for a face-to-face meeting to parents immediately. Likewise with any other information that makes the child feel uncomfortable.
- Never post a picture or any information online without informing a parent first.

In addition to children, there are a great number of adults who have been taken advantage of via the Internet. There are many sites out there that seek to either; solicit information in order to assume an identity, or attempt to solicit money for goods you may never receive, or both. Be wary of ordering goods from abroad; these entities do not have to conform to U.S. laws in many cases and are unregulated by our standards.

Often when you order goods or services on the Internet, the only form of accepted payment is a credit or debit card. It cannot be stressed enough that you should *never* use a debit card from your main checking account. You also should never use a credit card that has a high credit limit.

If you use a debit card from your primary checking account to order goods or services online and your account number is captured or otherwise compromised, it can create a financial disaster for you. If the identity thief begins to make charges on your account, more than likely it will cause an insufficient funds situation to occur due to other legitimate debits you have made. This will cause a domino effect that will only get worse as you try to fight the identity thief and your banking institution as well, which will want you to bring your account to balance sooner than later.

The same is true with a credit card that has a high limit. The identity thief or plain old thief who steals your account number will charge the maximum he or she can. The more such a person charges, the more you could be liable for, so it is best to use a card with a low limit (under $500), so if it is compromised, you know that is the most you would ever have to pay back. It should be stated that most legitimate credit card companies have fraud protections intended to prevent liability in these cases.

CASE STORY

Ann Nichols had been looking for a distinctive purse to have as an accessory to a new dress she had recently purchased. She had an upcoming event to which she wanted to wear the dress as well as the purse. She had been to all the local malls and women's stores, but nothing really caught her eye. One night, as she was browsing different Internet sites, she spotted the exact purse she wanted on sale for $300. It almost seemed too good to be true.

Ann was so excited about her find, she could hardly contain herself. She told her husband that she intended to order the purse and asked to use his card, which had a larger limit, to cover any shipping charges. The husband initially agreed, but when he saw that the vendor was a sole individual from China and not a company and realized the purse would have to be shipped from there, he became suspicious and told his wife no. Eager to go through with it, Ann calculated the price of the purse plus shipping charges and found that her card could handle the purchase.

Ann made the purchase and was told to allow at least four weeks for delivery. Ann eagerly waited. Five weeks later, Ann began to wonder why the purse never arrived. She went back online and looked up the vendor, who only listed an e-mail address as a point of contact. Ann sent the vendor a message and was told her purse had been sent out four weeks ago. When Ann informed the vendor via another message that she never got it, the vendor sent a reply that simply said, "Oh, well." Or in other words, *thanks for playing; you lose.* Ann was crushed and absolutely could not believe it but was powerless to do much except report the site.

Ann's story is mild compared to what can happen, but it serves to point out how easy it is to become a victim of Internet crime. *The Child/Adult Safety Bible* is about you not becoming a victim. Together, each of you who can read this book can help to put these scammers out of business.

CHAPTER 6

TRAVEL SECURITY

Millions of Americans travel each year for recreation as well as for business. With a growing number of travel-related accidents and incidents, it is more important to be mindful of travel safety than ever before. This chapter will offer the most basic of travel security tips and advice. It is the objective of this chapter to increase safety and awareness as it relates to travel security.

When you travel, you are actually more vulnerable to incident than you are in your own environment. You are exposed to more and different types of people, some who may have less-than-pure intentions. For that reason, it is good to know all you can to protect yourself against falling victim to ill-intentioned individuals.

There are many ideas and theories about safety and how to be safe. A search of the Internet will reveal many sites that feature individuals who are experts in one facet or another of safety. Most safety guidelines are basic; however, some are proactive in nature.

It is better to research a variety of safety basics like the ones offered in this book as well as others and choose the one that is best for you. For example, one set of safety rules may tell you that during a robbery, you should cooperate with the criminal and do as he asks. Another set of rules may advise you to look for an opportunity to run or fight. It is better to respond to a crisis based on your own ability. In the example given above, where the robber has you at gunpoint and could likely fire before you could take any action, it would be wise to be cooperative. At the same time, if he turns his head or lowers the weapon—*and* you are trained in how to safely disarm an armed suspect—then the odds may be better, but you are still at risk.

At the end of the day, the master of the decision is going to be the individual involved in the incident. The best thing you can do is have a good basis for your decision-making by doing all the research you can. Reading this book can be an important part of that research.

IN THE AIR

Before the 9/11 attacks, the standard procedure in the event of a hijacking was to just cooperate with the captors until their demands were met and the release of hostages was secured. Of course, after that event, all that changed. Now, a more proactive approach is suggested and is what is sometimes carried out by aircraft passengers at the first possible sign of trouble.

According to the Federal Aviation Administration's statistics on unruly passengers: As of September 8, 2008 there had already been 78 unruly passengers reported; in 2007, there were 147 reported, which is down slightly from the 304 that were reported in 2004. In 2001, there were 299 reported, some of whom we will always unfortunately remember.

In light of that, we can examine those numbers and realize that statistically, out of the thousands of flights per year, the numbers cited are not alarming. Despite the odds, it is possible that you could find yourself on a flight with an unruly passenger. In each critical incident, the more you know, the better off you are, in the air or on the ground.

Let's approach air safety from the ground up until you board the plane. In this day and age, almost anything can be used as a weapon, so regulations are even more limiting as to what is and is not allowed on the plane. Keep in mind what is and is not allowed on a plane constantly changes. Before flying you should go to the FAA website for the most current regulations. The following is a listing that was posted on the FAA website as of November of 2009:

Sporting Goods

Item	Carry-on	Checked
Baseball Bats	No	Yes
Bows and Arrows	No	Yes
Cricket Bats	No	Yes
Golf Clubs	No	Yes
Hockey Sticks	No	Yes
Lacrosse Sticks	No	Yes
Pool Cues	No	Yes
Ski Poles	No	Yes
Spear Guns	No	Yes

Guns & Firearms

Item	Carry-on	Checked
Ammunition—Check with your airline or travel agent to see if ammunition is permitted in checked baggage on the airline you are flying. If ammunition is permitted, it must be declared to the airline at check-in. Small arms ammunitions for personal use must be securely packed in fiber, wood or metal boxes or other packaging specifically designed to carry small amounts of ammunition. Ask about limitations or fees, if any, that apply.	No	Yes
BB guns	No	Yes
Compressed Air Guns (to include paintball markers)—Carried in checked luggage without compressed air cylinder attached.	No	Yes
Firearms—firearms carried as checked baggage MUST be unloaded, packed in a locked hard-sided container, and declared to the airline at check-in.	No	Yes
Flare Guns—May be carried as checked baggage MUST be unloaded, packed in a locked hard-sided container, and declared to the airline at check-in.	No	Yes

Item	Carry-on	Checked
Flares	No	No
Gun Lighters	No	Yes
Gun Powder including black powder and percussion caps	No	No
Parts of Guns and Firearms	No	Yes
Pellet Guns	No	Yes
Realistic Replicas of Firearms	No	Yes
Starter Pistols	No	Yes

NOTE: Check with your airline or travel agent to see if firearms are permitted in checked baggage on the airline you are flying. Ask about limitations or fees, if any, that apply.

Tools

Item	Carry-on	Checked
Axes and Hatchets	No	Yes
Cattle Prods	No	Yes
Crowbars	No	Yes
Hammers	No	Yes
Drills and drill bits (including cordless portable power drills)	No	Yes
Saws (including cordless portable power saws)	No	Yes
Tools (greater than seven inches in length)	No	Yes
Tools (seven inches or less in length)	Yes	Yes
Screwdrivers (seven inches or less in length)	Yes	Yes
Wrenches and Pliers (seven inches or less in length)	Yes	Yes

NOTE: Any sharp objects in checked baggage should be sheathed or securely wrapped to prevent injury to baggage handlers and Security Officers.

Martial Arts & Self-Defense Items

Item	Carry-on	Checked
Billy Clubs	No	Yes
Black Jacks	No	Yes
Brass Knuckles	No	Yes
Kubatons	No	Yes
Mace/Pepper Spray—One 118 ml or 4 fl. oz. container of mace or pepper spray is permitted in checked baggage, provided it is equipped with a safety mechanism to prevent accidental discharge. For more information visit *www.faa.gov;* click on Passengers, then Preparing to Fly.	No	Yes
Martial Arts Weapons	No	Yes
Night Sticks	No	Yes
Nunchakus	No	Yes
Stun Guns/Shocking Devices	No	Yes
Throwing Stars	No	Yes

NOTE: Any sharp objects in checked baggage should be sheathed or securely wrapped to prevent injury to baggage handlers and Security Officers.

Explosive & Flammable Materials, Disabling Chemicals & Other Dangerous Items

Explosive Materials	Carry-on	Checked
Blasting Caps	No	No
Dynamite	No	No
Fireworks	No	No
Flares (in any form)	No	No
Hand Grenades	No	No
Plastic Explosives	No	No
Realistic Replicas of Explosives	No	No
Flammable Items	**Carry-on**	**Checked**
Aerosol (any except for personal care or toiletries in limited quantities)	No	No

	Carry-on	Checked
Fuels (including cooking fuels and any flammable liquid fuel)	No	No
Gasoline	No	No
Gas Torches	No	No
Lighter Fluid	No	No
Common Lighters - Lighters without fuel are permitted in checked baggage. Lighters with fuel are prohibited in checked baggage, unless they adhere to the Department of Transportation (DOT) exemption, which allows up to two fueled lighters if properly enclosed in a DOT-approved case. If you are uncertain as to whether your lighter is prohibited, please leave it at home.	Yes	No
Torch Lighters—Torch lighters create a thin, needle-like flame that is hotter (reaching 2,500 degrees Fahrenheit) and more intense than those from common lighters. Torch lighters are often used for pipes and cigars, and maintain a consistent stream of air-propelled fire regardless of the angle at which it is held. Torch lighters continue to be banned.	No	No
Strike-anywhere Matches—One book of safety (non-strike anywhere) matches are permitted as carry-on items, but all matches are prohibited in checked baggage.	No	No
Flammable Paints (See Other Items below for non-flammable paints)	No	No
Turpentine and Paint Thinner	No	No
Realistic Replicas of Incendiaries	No	No

NOTE: There are other hazardous materials that are regulated by the FAA. This information is summarized at *www.faa.gov,* click on Passengers, then Preparing to Fly.

Disabling Chemicals & Other Dangerous Items	Carry-on	Checked
Chlorine for Pools and Spas	No	No

Small compressed gas cartridges (Up to 2 in life vests and 2 spares)	Yes	Yes
Fire extinguishers and other compressed gas cylinders	No	No
Liquid Bleach	No	No
Spillable Batteries—except those in wheelchairs	No	No
Spray Paint	No	No
Tear Gas	No	No

NOTE: There are other hazardous materials that are regulated by the FAA. This information is summarized at *www.faa.gov.*

Other Items

Item	Carry-on	Checked
Gel-type candles	No	Yes
Gel shoe inserts—Gel shoe inserts are not permitted, but shoes constructed with gel heels are allowed and must be removed and screened.	No	Yes
Non-flammable liquid, gel, or aerosol paint	Yes - 3 oz. or smaller container	Yes
Flammable liquid, gel, or aerosol paint	No	No
Snow globes and like decorations regardless of size or amount of liquid inside, even with documentation.	No	Yes

Posted on: *www.tsa.gov/Prohibited items*

To the untrained eye, some of what is prohibited for carrying onto the aircraft may not make much sense at first glance. Thanks to extensive research by officials, it has been found that some of these items can be either used as weapons or used to make weapons. We won't go into exactly how this can be done, but we will acknowledge that most, if not all, of the items listed could be dangerous in some way.

Defensive Travel

When you make your reservation, never use your official title if you have one; list only Mr. or Ms. and your first and last name, what you list will have to match your identification or travel documents. Potential travelers should always research current regulations before flight. If given a choice in seating, it is recommended a window or a seat in the rear of the aircraft is selected; in the event of a hijacking, this will keep you further away from whatever action is taking place. A window seat near an emergency exit is probably the best seat you can have under these circumstances; in some rare situations, it could even provide an opportunity for escape.

When you arrive at the airport, be cognizant and alert of any suspicious behavior. Be aware of any suspicious or unattended baggage or packages. Be ready to report to security personnel anything that does not look right. Never investigate a suspicious situation yourself; you could make a bad situation worse in several ways. Even an off-duty law-enforcement officer should defer to airport security; airport personnel are specially trained in dealing with security issues inside the airport.

In general, there are two types of attacks that may be carried out: against an aircraft or its passengers. The plane may be directly attacked in order to kill as many people as possible, or the plane may be hijacked and demands may be made by the captors.

Direct attack

In the event of an attack, try to go to the nearest cover. Remember cover only hides you from view but will not stop a projectile. Avoid running for too long, as an individual running will draw the attention of an attacker. If you must move, stay low and go from cover to cover, tucking your arms and elbows next to your ribcage to protect your heart, lungs, and chest in case of flying projectiles. Responding security personnel will not be able to distinguish you from the attackers, so make no attempt to assist them in any way and remain still until told to move.

Hijacking

As stated earlier, the common wisdom before the 9/11 attacks was to cooperate with the hijackers until a safe conclusion could be reached by negotiators on the ground. It was thought that all hijackers wanted something; all that had to be done, therefore, was to identify what that was and negotiate for the safe release of the hostages. Another approach was to buy time until security forces could take them out.

In the event of a hijacking, the proper response today is likely to be much different. It will depend on the individual situation, but in most cases, a proactive approach will be in the thoughts and minds of all aboard the aircraft.

Plane Crash

Some statistics show that two-thirds of people involved in a plane crash survive, and perhaps one-third of the people who die might have survived if they had taken certain precautions. We in no way mean to suggest that, in general, plane crashes are survivable. The truth is when a plane crashes, it is a very dangerous situation, not only for the passengers but for anyone in the area where the plane goes down.

We only hope to relay a few safety precautions that can be taken in the event of a crash, to give you every opportunity to survive.

- When you enter a plane, make note of all the emergency exits. This will be very helpful if there is no light after a crash and you need to exit the plane.

- When you are seated and told to secure the seatbelt around you, make sure that it is both snug and secure. It may be more comfortable to leave slack in the belt, but that is not safe in the event of a crash.

- If possible, remove sharp objects from your person. This would include pens, pencils, eyeglasses, high-heeled shoes, and dentures. In the event of a crash, these items can cause injury to you. If you don't need these items during the flight, secure them in a briefcase until you land.

- You should carry on any medication you may need for a twenty-four-hour period. If you are flying through any areas that might present cold weather, be sure to pack a warm sweater or coat in your carry-on luggage. In the event you survive a crash, these items will be useful until you are rescued.

- Try to empty your bladder before the flight if possible; in the event of a crash, a full bladder increases your chance of internal injury.

- In the event of smoke during or after a crash, wet a handkerchief, shirttail, or cloth of some kind and hold it over your mouth. This should only be done if it is the only thing available to you. The steam from the wet towel could cause issues but it may be better than breathing smoke.

- If you know a crash is imminent, go ahead and place a pillow in your lap and assume the crash position demonstrated by the flight attendants at the beginning of the flight. To get proper details on the position, pay close attention to the safety lecture and follow the instructions of the airline staff when you are flying.

Historically, some passengers have survived the initial crash, only to die later from events that occur after the crash. After a crash, the plane may catch on fire and fill with smoke. The flight attendants may be stunned or otherwise incapacitated. It is imperative that you maintain your composure and exit the plane immediately via the closest available exit. Of course, this will not be as easy as it may sound; there will also be other panicked passengers trying to exit quickly as well. Try to stand straight up and move with the flow of the group, to reduce your chance of being trampled. Once you exit, get as far away from the wreckage as possible.

ON THE ROAD

In 2004, The World Health Organization (WHO) estimated that 1.2 million people are killed and 50 million injured every year due to road accidents worldwide. What is difficult to estimate is how many of these accidents could have been avoided.

When traveling, you generally have to worry about two things: *travel safety* and *travel security*. Travel safety is just being safe and exercising good, sound practices in order to arrive at your destination. Travel security is protecting yourself while on the road from others who may wish to take advantage of you.

The term *travel safety* is a generic one; it refers to taking common sense precautions and actions: "Always wear your seatbelt" and "keep your eyes on the road at all times" are examples. Not doing these things and taking your eyes off the road for any reason can cause more accidents and injuries than you think or could estimate. Since travel safety usually involves practices that everyone knows but fails to follow, we won't spend a lot of time on it. The following are just some basic general travel safety tips.

- Don't block the passing lane.

- Don't tailgate.

- If you are traveling slower than normal or having difficulty, pull over and allow faster traffic to pass.

- Stay away from erratic or aggressive drivers.

- Don't challenge other drivers by speeding up to hold a position.

- Ignore obscene gestures; do not return them.

- Do not stop in the roadway for any reason.

- Try not to pull over on the shoulder of the road, but if you must do so, get as far off the roadway as you can.

- If you have car trouble and a stranger approaches, remain in your car and ask the stranger to call for help.

- Keep your eyes on the road.

- Always use your seatbelt.

Travel security is of great concern these days. There are many individuals who seek to take advantage of travelers. When you think about it, you are actually very vulnerable when you travel; you are out of your normal environment and familiar surroundings.

On average, two cars are stolen every minute somewhere in the United States. A large percentage of these have the doors unlocked or keys in the ignition. Just like accidents, many car thefts can be avoided by simply properly securing the vehicle. The following are general steps to secure your vehicle that may save you a lot of grief later. The most important thing about any security measures is that you must practice them every time. Thieves, abusers, kidnappers, and rapists are opportunistic criminals; this means that if you provide them with an opportunity, they will strike.

- Never leave valuables visible on the seat or dash of your car.

- Roll your windows all the way up when you exit your vehicle.

- Avoid hiding spare keys on the vehicle; if you must carry a spare, keep it on your person, in your pocket or shoe.

- Try to park in areas that have heavy foot or auto traffic passing by.

- Try to park in well-lit areas if possible.

- When you exit the vehicle, have keys in hand and be ready to make a quick re-entry if needed.

- Always lock your doors; if you have keyless entry, make it a habit to listen for the chirp or click of the doors locking.

- Put special markings on valuables to make them more identifiable if stolen and recovered.

- When returning to your vehicle, have your keys in hand and ready so there is no hesitation in getting into your vehicle.

- Be mindful of what or who may be under your vehicle.

- Before you get in your vehicle, always glance at the back seat.

Your vehicle is the backbone of your road travel; if something happens to it, your whole trip will be compromised. You are also more vulnerable to other threats when you have car trouble or your car is stolen. When considering vehicle security, the best thought to keep in mind is that while you may not be able to prevent your vehicle from becoming a statistic, you can make it a little more difficult for a would-be thief or other opportunist.

With Children

Traveling on a road trip with children presents a whole new set of challenges. The recommendations are not much different from what they would be if you were at home (which we have already covered). The most important modification would be that when on the road and traveling with children, it is best not to ever let them out of your sight, even to go to the restroom. If possible, arrange to go to the restroom with them when you stop at a rest area or convenience store. John Walsh, the host of *America's Most Wanted,* a popular crime television program, has survived every parent's worst nightmare; his son Adam disappeared within minutes of leaving his mother to go to another part of a store. As we all know he was later killed presumably by the abductor. This unfortunate incident serves as an example of how quickly things can happen—and when you least expect it.

No one wants to be a victim, but with so many criminal opportunists out there, unfortunately you have to take measures to reduce your chances of becoming victimized. If you don't protect yourself, who will?

Women Traveling Alone

Criminals are opportunistic and don't follow society's rules. They see women and children as weaker victims upon whom they can easily prey.

The most basic example of this is when a younger person goes to a car dealership to purchase a car. Commonly, the salesman's approach will be different when dealing with such an individual than it would be with an older man looking at the same vehicle. The thing is, some teenagers, young adults, and women are very knowledgeable about cars. The salesman simply prejudges them and thinks that he can take advantage of his assumption about their suspected lack of knowledge. The same is true of the criminal opportunist who thinks that he can take advantage of people based on their gender, age, or appearance. The goal of this book is to prepare the individual, so just like the car salesman, the criminal opportunist will also be mistaken when he sees a individual he feels is unprepared.

Through the author's independent study of general human behavior, it has been noted that some people simply don't pay attention to their surroundings. In some cases, a potential attacker will watch his victim for a long period of time before he actually attacks. The attacker may be trying to assess if the potential victim is alone, what her habits are, and what places she frequents. In some cases, a potential attacker may watch for hours or even days before he strikes. For this reason, it is important to be aware of your surroundings. Make note of people who may seem to give you a second glance. Be aware if you move to a different location within the area and run into the same individual again. Make a mental note of what he is wearing, and be able to describe him if necessary.

In today's society, some people are taught not to look at or acknowledge strangers in any way. They are taught that paying no attention is the safe thing to do. From a safety standpoint, this is just not a good idea. Just like with any other potential problem, ignoring it will not make it go away; in fact, it may only make it worse. Acknowledge and pay attention to the actions of every stranger, especially those who seem to be watching you. The fact that you make it clear you see them watching you and are not happy about it conveys a type of confidence that may deter some criminal opportunists. These opportunists sometimes rely on the belief that you don't notice them watching you. This gives them the element of surprise. When you notice them watching you, you take that element away from them.

How you carry yourself can often make all the difference in the world. As stated earlier, a potential attacker looks to prey on someone he feels may be weak. Try not to project a weak image; walk upright and with confidence. When traveling, try to appear as if you know where you are going—even if you are lost. Practice your poker face; never let fear or unsure feelings translate to the expression on your face.

In many cases, a situation you perceive to be a threat may be little more than a harmless initial romantic interest. Even at that, it is important to be aware of it initially. That way, you will know the very minute it appears to turn into something more serious or dangerous than that. The best rule is to use precaution until you learn what a person's motives are.

TAKING ACTION

> *"Never leave fate to chance waiting on others to act. Act*
> *in your own favor and on your own behalf."*
> -Cory B. Harris

Unfortunately, there are times where you may have to take action when attacked or threatened. This is always a personal choice and should be weighed with the proper care and tailored to the individual. What you are about to read here are suggestions for times when you may have to make a life-or-death choice. It is up to you to ponder and take the best action for yourself, should a situation arise where you are under attack or the threat of attack.

In general, you want to defend yourself at the point of attack. An attacker often prefers to take the victim to a secondary location to do harm. This is especially true in the case of rapists and abductors. If an abductor attempts to force you in his car, the most recommended course of action (not just by us but by most security experts) is to make as much noise as you can and do everything you can to avoid being put into his vehicle. This is advised if you are being abducted in a public place. In most cases, the abductor wants to get you to a private place where no one can hear you at all. At that time, he can do to you whatever he wants to do without fear of discovery.

Keep in mind that we are talking about an attack or abduction scenario, not an armed robbery. In the case of an armed robbery, the proper response is different. In these cases, if the robber gets what he demands, he may not hurt you. In these cases, it may be best to simply give him what he is asking for. Material things can always be replaced, but you have only one life. It is best to part with the material possessions in this case. The best thing to remember in these cases is to do what you can to ensure the best possible chance of your survival. Sometimes the answer may be to run, and other times, it may be to scream or alert others, and in some cases you may have to comply. You have to weigh each situation as it unfolds and choose the option that you feel comfortable with.

Of course, an attempted abduction or rape may be the worst-case scenario you may encounter while traveling. Again, our goal is to reduce the chances of you becoming a victim. Let us now examine some general precautions that may help you avoid getting into the situation we just examined in the first place.

- **Be alert in parking lots**

When you are going to your car at night, do not hesitate to ask for an escort if one is available. If you must go alone, make sure you have your keys out and ready, and take the most direct route to your vehicle. Look around and be very aware of your surroundings as you approach your vehicle. Before you get in, always glance in the back seat of your vehicle.

- **Pulling over once in transit at the behest of a stranger**

Once you leave the area, if a stranger pulls up alongside you and motions to you, to indicate something may be wrong with your car, thank him kindly and proceed to the nearest well-populated and well-lit gas station to check it out. If the stranger continues to follow you, be prepared to call 911 or just go to the nearest police station. Pulling over on the side of the road could be dangerous in this case and should not be done.

- **Locking your car doors**

As soon as you enter your vehicle, the first thing you should do is lock your car doors. This way, if you make an unexpected stop (such as for a stop sign or traffic light), an attacker would have to defeat the locking mechanism before he could gain access to you inside your car. This may afford you the proper time you need to act.

- **Trusting an honest-looking or clean-cut stranger**

Stereotyping a person based on looks has always been a bad way to judge character, but for years, it's been done. When it comes to your safety, use precaution when you encounter anyone you don't know. Don't accept a ride from a stranger based on how he looks. Ted Bundy, one of the most dangerous and prolific serial killers America has ever seen, gained access to his victims because he didn't look like a "bad guy" to his victims at first. Most thought he was a nice guy and trusted him initially. By most accounts, he was classified as a clean-cut, well-mannered individual.

- **Becoming too routine**

A good daily routine usually brings stability and ease to one's life, but in the case of personal safety, it can be a liability. If you are ever the subject of a stalker or a run-of-the-mill thief who seeks to catch you slipping, routine can be your enemy.

Vary the times you leave for work in the morning. If possible, leave a little earlier than you normally would. Change the route you take to your destination one or two times a week. When possible, come home for lunch, so you don't develop the routine of being gone all day once you leave in the morning. If you jog for your health, by all means, change the times and routes you use.

At the end of the day, you have to remember that public servants are there to serve and protect you, but you first have to take action to protect yourself. Help is usually five or ten minutes away at best, so it is crucial to take precaution whenever and wherever you can.

CHAPTER 7

SECURING HOME AND FAMILY

In all likelihood, your home contains your most prized material possessions. It is a place where you can relax, let your guard down, and rest. Most importantly, it is the place where your family lives and sleeps at night. With that in mind, securing it is very important.

There are a number of threats to the home front. Since the home is often viewed as a place of relaxation, it is easy to overlook security measures at your home. In this chapter, we will discuss some of the things you can do to secure your home and family. What we will suggest will be universal precautions, by which we mean that no matter where you live or in what neighborhood you live, you can apply what is discussed in your own household. Crime knows no status or standing; anyone can be a victim, but while there are actions you can take to lower your risk, there are never any guarantees.

Home-intrusion robberies

One of the most dangerous threats to your home is the home-intrusion robbery. In this type of robbery, armed suspects enter your home while you and your family are actually there. This is not to be confused with a burglary, which is what happens when a criminal enters your home when you are away, for the purposes of taking items that belong to you.

For obvious reasons, a home-intrusion robbery is very dangerous; your family is exposed to grave bodily danger. The criminals have the same goals in both a burglary and a home intrusion—they want to take valuable items that belong to you—but the presence of your family at home during the crime presents other dangers.

The suspects may not want to leave any witnesses behind to call police. In addition to being thieves, the suspects could also be rapists or pedophiles, which poses an additional threat to any women and children in the house. Statistics suggest that any neighborhood can be hit by one of these type of robberies; the more affluent the area, the more likely it may be—after all, it makes no sense for the poor to rob from the poor. A thief is going to rob from a place he thinks has something valuable inside.

Now that we have outlined the dangers, let us discuss what can be done to lower your chances of being victimized by this type of robbery.

- When you enter your home, always lock the door behind you, even if you intend to go back out later; you never know who is watching.

- Restrict the number of people who have keys to your home. If a key is lost or misplaced, change the locks immediately. Also, when you first move into a previously occupied home, for obvious reasons you should change the locks first thing. You have no way of knowing who has keys to those locks.

- Weapons are a personal choice, but if you choose to have them in your home, they could be helpful in the event of a home-intrusion robbery. The weapon should be kept in a secure area that is also readily assessable by you. Limit the access to and knowledge of this weapon's location.

- Be alert to workmen in the area and refuse any unordered package that may arrive at your home.

- Don't hesitate to write down license plate numbers of suspicious vehicles and make mental note of any suspicious persons you may observe.

The only real difference between a "good" neighborhood and a "bad" one is the extent to which the neighbors will get involved. The common belief is that the best neighborhoods are the ones with the highest socioeconomic status. In the author's opinion; regardless of the earning potential of the occupants of a neighborhood, crime flourishes best in areas that are gripped by fear. When individuals who live in an area are afraid to get involved, report crimes, write down the plates of suspicious vehicles, call in suspicious activity, and otherwise remain vigilant, everyone knows it—especially criminals.

Neighborhood watches have been set up in crime-ridden areas and have been very successful in the past. The difference between people who will accept crime and people who come together to decide they won't take it anymore is enormous. Even where there is not an organized neighborhood watch, a collection of concerned citizens can do a world of good. After all, a thief is unlikely to burglarize a house if he feels like the neighbors who live beside that house will call police.

There is always safety in numbers. The more people you have on board in the area where you live, the better off you are. This book is designed to advise an individual who may only have himself or herself to rely on, so it will focus on what you can do, as opposed to what others can do for you.

More important than any material possession you may have are the lives of yourself and your family. No one can fully control what can and may happen. You can only take all the precaution you know how, to keep your family safe; at the end of the day, that is all any man or woman can do. Surely everyone has the desire to do what is right but maybe not the full knowledge of what to do. No one knows everything, but what you are reading here is a sharing of ideas. Much of it is common sense, but this book may contain a few new ideas for you.

Some of the following has been previously stated, but it bears repeating:

- Instruct children to keep doors and windows locked and deny admittance to strangers at all times.

- Show children how to summon police and other emergency

services to your home. They should also know their address at the earliest possible age it can be taught.

- If you have to leave children at home alone, make sure you leave your home well lit and instruct your children that they are not allowed to use the stove or any other potentially dangerous appliance while unsupervised.

- Teach your children that they are not to leave the house without asking your permission, and advising you where they are going, and who they are going to meet.

- Have your children travel in pairs or groups.

- Instruct your children to report any suspicious contact with strangers.

With all that has been said about securing the family, don't forget that you also have to secure the structure itself first. There are plenty of products that can be purchased to make your home more secure, including improved locks, sturdier windows, and various alarms and surveillance systems. Unfortunately, not all doors, locks, and windows are created equal; some provide more protection than others. To ensure that you invest your money wisely when considering home-security upgrades, consult your local police department. Many departments have a crime-prevention specialist who can advise which locks, doors, and alarm systems fit your situation.

You should choose solid-wood outer doors for your home with a deadbolt lock independent of a locking doorknob. If you install an alarm, make sure you place the contacts on all rear windows and doors, in addition to the main entrance—rear windows and doors are more likely to be a point of entry for thieves.

Bars on windows and doors are a personal choice; they will definitely aid in keeping people out, but at the same time, in case of emergency, they can also make it more difficult for your family to get out quickly. Weigh heavily the pros and cons of bars before installing them. Control vegetation around these entryways for optimal visibility. Plants and shrubs around a home may look decorative for some but can aid criminals by providing cover around your door. Along those same lines, you should have good lighting around your residence. In the same way shrubs can provide cover for criminals, so can shadow.

For safety reasons, have a basic first aid kit and at least two fire extinguishers in the home. If you have dangerous animals that could bite trespassers, go ahead and post a warning sign where it can be seen.

In closing, when it comes to securing your home and family; there is only what works for you and your family that is most important. If you can think of things beyond what has been listed here, by all means employ them if they work for you. When it comes to safety, remember that there are some things you can control, and that includes deciding what will work for you. You are encouraged to do all you can.

DOMESTIC BATTERY
(The Threat From Within)

Domestic violence is a dangerous family situation that often results in serious injury or death. In addition to the threat to the family members involved, it has also caused the death of many police officers who were responding to calls for assistance.

Often referred to as domestic battery, which is generally the legal term for this type of family violence, the words domestic violence is sometimes used to describe the same act.

Battery is defined as the intentional, harmful, or offensive touching of another person without their consent (Merriam-Webster 2011). If this type of touching occurs without the victim's permission or consent, under the law, it is classified as a battery. When this type of touching involves family members who are related by blood or marriage, live together in the same home, or have (in some states) dated, it is charged under the law as domestic battery of either the first, second, or third degree.

Criminal codes for domestic battery are different from state to state. For example, in some states, violence between people who have dated but never lived together or been married can be charged as domestic violence. In other states, it may not meet the threshold requirements to be charged as such. In order for a police officer to charge a potential suspect with domestic battery, certain acts or elements will have to take place. It is important that the officer weigh the elements heavily, because the charge will almost always be challenged in court later, often by the suspect and sometimes by the victim. In countless cases, suspect and victim will have reunited and resumed their relationship before the case goes to court.

Just to give you an example, the following is the *Arkansas* criminal code for domestic battering in the third degree:

5-26-305. Domestic battering in the third degree

(a) A person commits domestic battering in the third degree if:

(1) With the purpose of causing physical injury to a family or household member, a person causes physical injury to a family or household member, or

(2) A person recklessly causes physical injury to a family or household member, or;

(3) A person negligently causes physical injury to a family or household member by means of a deadly weapon; or

(4) A person purposely causes stupor, unconsciousness, or physical or mental impairment or injury or injury to a family or household member by administering to a family or household member, with the family or household member's consent, any drug or other substance.

(b)(1) Domestic battering in the third degree is a Class A misdemeanor.

The way the law is written is very important; it affects who is charged, when, and why they are charged.

In the author's professional opinion, the law should be written in a gender-neutral manner, in the interest of fairness. Though the majority of offenders are men, there are cases where women have committed this offense as well. The law should be applied as equally as possible according to the evidence.

A good solid domestic violence law will have certain elements that must be met before a physical on-scene arrest can occur. There should be some sign of physical injury in the victim or some sign that a battery has occurred. The direct evidence would be bruising, cuts, broken bones, or bleeding wounds from the victim. If the victim has no visible injuries but is making a claim that a battery has occurred, indirect evidence such as disheveled hair or torn clothing may be considered. An examination of the area where the battery was alleged to have occurred may yield even more.

Is the furniture turned and tossed or in disarray? Are pictures knocked off the wall?

It is common practice in some states that a suspect in a domestic battery can be arrested solely off the word of the alleged victim. This is done in an abundance of caution, to ensure that the alleged violence does not escalate into something more serious. While it is understandable why an arrest may be made in this manner, legally it may not always be the best practice, because it invites abuse of the law; when this is known, any person can allege anything against another person in order to have them arrested, with no proof at all that a crime has been committed. Even in felony arrest, there normally has to be some evidence other than the sole word of one person for an arrest to be made.

The laws vary from state to state as to when and how this crime is charged. Getting the offender arrested is only half the battle; there is bond and pre-trial release that the victim will have to contend with, during which the offender is back out on the street.

The goal is to keep yourself safe if you are a victim. Unfortunately, many measures that can be used as protection in these situations have to be undertaken by the victim. The police are not counselors, doctors, lawyers, or personal security officers. Although police are sometimes used as all these things and more, they have only one real power: the power to arrest. Once that is utilized, then the legal system takes over. In essence, if violence in the household is a real problem, an arrest is only a temporary fix. It will solve the problem for a few days or weeks but does not even begin to address some long-term issues.

Often, if family violence is going to be an issue, it becomes apparent long before it escalates to the point where police are called. Often the first sign that violence will occur begins with the offender trying to control the victim. The attempt to control may then escalate to verbal abuse, manipulation, and general mischief. Soon the offender will seek to enforce his or her control through physical violence.

At the first sign of violence, the ideal course of action for the victim is to get away or leave the situation. As simple as it sounds, for reasons that are very hard to explain, this rarely happens; these situations tend to linger and go on for months and sometimes years. The truth is that it is easier to leave at the first sign of difficulty than it is later on. In the first stages, a couple may only be dating. They may not be living together, and they may not have any children yet. It is far easier to make a change before these things occur than it is after, but even later, it is still not *impossible* by any stretch.

It cannot be stressed enough that the best course of action that will work is to leave the situation in most cases. Often a victim is his or her own worst enemy in these situations. In many cases, there were clear warning signs long before injury or death occurs, but the victim either stayed in the situation too long or returned to the situation after he or she had left. These decisions are often led by emotion, fear, or a perceived financial dependence, rather than sound reasoning. As hard as it may be, the most important thing the victim can do is sever emotional ties and make decisions based on what is better for him or her and any children who may be involved.

When the fear of leaving is based on perceived financial independence, you need only ask yourself, "Is the financial stability worth my life?" In all cases, the answer is no; there is no amount of money or financial stability worth the lives of yourself or your children. It may require that you dig deep within yourself, but in situations where you may be subjected to violence, you have to do what is best to keep yourself safe. In most cases, that involves getting yourself and your children out of the situation.

When we began to research domestic violence, we found the number of victims who remained in the situation which ultimately led to their injury or death was staggering. In many cases, we found that there was no need for these victims to have been injured or killed. Both could have been avoided, had they left their abuser at the first sign of violence. Since the most common reason for not leaving such a situation may be perceived financial stability, let us examine a few things. First, we will list a few resources that can be utilized to help a person get out of a domestic violence situation.

- Domestic Abuse Hotline 1-888-743-5754
- Local domestic violence shelters
- Friends

- Family
- Church
- Pastors
- Legal Aid
- Local domestic violence intervention/advocacy group
- Domestic violence unit of your local police department

The previous list is not exhaustive regarding what is actually out there. An Internet search will reveal more specifically what is out there in your particular geographic area, and explain how you can contact them. What we listed here are common resources that are available in most communities. With all that is available, the decision to stay in a bad situation is often more of an excuse than a need.

Domestic abuse shelters are good when there are few other resources. The location is usually never revealed in some cases (even to police), but there is usually a phone number listed in the phone book for the facility. This is an excellent resource if the victim needs security and secrecy from the offender. These facilities generally charge the victim nothing, and lodging and food are provided for the victim and any children the victim may have. There are a number of hotlines that provide assistance to victims; we only listed one of them, but there are many more than that. The professionals who answer the phone can provide almost any information the victim may need and direct them to local facilities that may be of assistance.

In many families, there is usually at least one family member who is willing to help; don't be afraid to utilize family and friends who have expressed interest in helping you get out of the situation. The same is true with pastors and church congregations; both are excellent resources that often have a system already in place to assist.

If you are afraid of violence at home, it is always good to have a protection plan in place. Nothing you can plan is foolproof, but it is good to have some sort of plan in place to assist you when you find yourself in a bad situation.

The potential victim should always attempt to secure whatever legal protections the law will allow. This could include an order of protection, stay-away orders, restraining orders, or criminal trespass notifications. Most communities have public legal aid departments that will often assist free of charge. In addition, the police should be notified every time the offender contacts them or shows up uninvited at the victim's place of residence or work. This type of paper trail is vital in showing a pattern of harassment or abuse by the offender. Any call the police respond to is always documented and can be recalled at a later date.

At the first sign that there may be trouble in the relationship, try to put some money away for emergencies, in case you have to leave in a hurry. In the beginning, start by putting away enough for one night's motel stay and then work up from there and add to it every time you can. There is nothing dishonest about this; it's never a bad idea to save money whenever you can. You never know when you may need some accessible cash.

The next thing to do is have a trusted friend or family member you can call anytime. Have a code word established with this person that will clearly communicate that you are in immediate danger and need help right away. The potential victim need only speak the word over the phone; then the friend will know to call police.

Just to focus you on how real family violence is, below are a few condensed stories of incidents that we thought were significant, names have been withheld of course.

CASE 1

Girlfriend and boyfriend are living toether after a one-year courtship. The girlfriend has one child, a four-year-old daughter from a previous relationship. After about six months, the couple's relationship slowly begins to turn volatile. Soon the boyfriend begins to assault the girlfriend, and they fight often. Each day, the girlfriend leaves her child with the boyfriend—often after these fights or arguments—and goes to work.

In the beginning, the girlfriend notices some minor bruising on the little girl but accepts the boyfriend's explanation that these happened while the child was playing. One day, the child dies while home alone with the boyfriend he is slow to call for an ambulance. By the time help arrives, the child is dead on the scene. The boyfriend claims that the child fell while playing and hit her head. It is unknown exactly what has happened—until an autopsy reveals that the child died from a blow to the head consistent with being struck in the head with a hard, blunt object. The child had suffered a skull fracture as well as a fracture on her arm and multiple bruising, some of which were old wounds. The boyfriend is arrested and eventually is sentenced to do time in prison.

In this case, there are several questions to ask:

- What went wrong?
- What could have been done differently or better?
- Were there any signs that something awful would happen?

In answer to the last question, yes, there were. In addition to what you read in the narrative, the boyfriend routinely refused to open the door when he was alone with the child and other relatives came over to check on the child. In this case, no one really knows exactly what happened in the home, but it appears the boyfriend may have taken out his anger and frustrations on the child when the mother left.

Who you leave your children with is always a personal choice, but it's common sense to limit the number of people whom you entrust to watch over your child. Remember, simply being in a relationship with someone does not automatically qualify them to be a responsible or safe caregiver for your child.

CASE 2

Michael and Connie had been dating about nine years, off and on. Michael hit Connie from time to time. He has never caused any serious injuries, but the abuse has always been a constant in their relationship. At times, Connie thought of leaving, but Michael would apologize and promise to seek counseling. One time, Michael attended three counseling sessions with Connie to address problems of abuse. Connie was always optimistic that things would improve, and with time invested, she didn't want to give up on the relationship.

Connie and Michael continued to date, and the arguing slowly became even more frequent and more intense. Usually at the height of his anger was when Michael would strike her, and it was almost always in the head, either closed- or open-handed. This would usually bring an end to the argument, as Connie didn't want to fight back. She wasn't interested in calling the police, so she would simply retreat back into herself so the violence would stop. This always worked, after the initial blow; Michael would say a few more angry words and then go away, still angry, but Connie rationalized, he never followed up with a second blow.

One day, Michael and Connie got into an argument while spending an evening at Michael's home. Something was different about this argument; Michael seemed angrier than ever before. He stated that he was tired of Connie's actions and that he was going to put an end to it. This time, Connie sensed something was different with Michael, so instead of sticking around until she was struck, she simply ran outside and got in her car. She drove toward her own residence.

After Connie had traveled about a mile, her cell phone rang. It was Michael. He was still angry but demanded that Connie turn around and come back so they could talk. Against her better judgment, Connie turned around and headed back to go talk to Michael. Michael met her in the front yard, where they continued to argue. Michael, as usual, drew back and struck Connie in the head, as she was standing on the top step of Michael's porch. She fell, struck her head on the concrete, and was rendered unconscious.

Michael ran and left Connie there without summoning any aid. Fortunately, a neighbor saw the whole incident occur and called an ambulance. Connie was rushed to the hospital with head trauma and internal bleeding; she was unresponsive to initial treatments eight hours after being admitted to the emergency room.

****

Much can be learned from this story, which lends credence to the theory that by getting out of a bad situation quickly, you are better off. Historically these types of situations only escalate; they rarely de-escalate. A potential victim should keep that in mind from the first very moment of the very first blow he or she receives. If an individual ever acts like he or she will strike you or says that he or she wants to hurt you, it would be in your best interest to take the person seriously.

The second point is to recognize that Connie made the right choice to leave the scene when it appeared that things may escalate. Of course, it was unwise to return; you should never go back to a situation that is swelling with anger. Trust your instincts and leave—and stay away—when you feel threatened. Your first instinct to leave is the right one. In most cases, even the police encourage someone to leave the scene when they answer a domestic abuse call, if they don't have enough evidence to make an arrest. This is done in order to allow for some cooling off; it is hoped that as anger subsides, rational thinking will return.

CASE 3

Late on a Friday night, a police officer is on patrol. He receives a call about a domestic battery in progress. The officer has handled many of these before in his short career. It seemed to be an everyday thing; officers handled at least one of these per shift. The officer acknowledged receipt of the call and proceeded to the address.

Once he arrived on scene, the officer could hear the arguing from outside the home. The officer knew backup was just minutes away, so he decided to go on in and begin to calm the situation and gather information. Unfortunately, as soon as the officer walked through the door, he was immediately shot by the male suspect who was involved in the domestic disturbance. The officer died instantly from the wound he received.

It is commonly known that a domestic disturbance is by far the most dangerous call an officer can answer. When an officer (or anyone else, for that matter) walks through the door, it is unknown exactly what will be found on the other side of it. This story ended badly and multiple lives were affected.

- The officer is dead, leaving behind any children, wife, or parents still living.

- The suspect is headed to jail for the rest of his life (or may even be killed by the other officers if he does not surrender).

- The wife he was arguing with (and any children they may have) will suffer a loss, but if one is looking for a silver lining, his family is most likely safer when he is no longer in the home.

CASE 4

John and Karen have been a couple for four years. During this time, they have had their ups and downs but are really fond of each other. John is very easygoing and laid back. Karen is more outgoing, spontaneous, and unpredictable

Lately, the couple has been arguing because John has been working late, and Karen believes he is seeing another woman. Karen has always been very jealous and somewhat insecure throughout the relationship. John has always done a good job of making her feel secure by calling when he was going to be late and opting to stay home rather than go out with friends several times.

Karen finds little comfort in John's attempts to make her feel better. She often gets angry when he doesn't answer his cell phone and when he has to work late. Karen often throws dishes at John when she is angry. When this happens, John usually leaves the house and simply returns after she has calmed down.

One particular night, John comes home late from work tired and goes straight to bed. This raises Karen's suspicions, and she rifles through John's pockets while he is asleep. She finds a piece of paper in his pocket with "Jennifer" and a phone number listed on it. Karen becomes very angry, thinking that this explains his absence on all those late nights when he said he was at work. She grows furious, convinced that John has been lying to her all this time. Karen subsequently allows her anger to get the best of her. She goes into the kitchen, grabs a knife, and enters the room where John is sleeping. She stabs him six times in the back.

In shock at what she has done, she calls no one and sits on the couch until the next morning. The phone rings at about 6:30 AM, and Karen answers it, ready to go ahead and tell anyone on the other end what she has done. When she picks up the phone and says hello, the voice on the other end says, "Hello, this is Jennifer Smith. I'm John's new supervisor.

He was supposed to report to me at 6:00 AM for his new assignment. He was transferred to me yesterday. I'm calling to make sure he is okay."

****

Not much can be added here, except to say that things are not always what they seem—and that even if they are, it is not worth a person's life.

Unfortunately, domestic battery is responsible for many deaths every year, as we have indicated. The bare basics of protecting yourself start with following your instincts:

- If the situation seems bad, it probably is.

- If something tells you that you should leave, you probably should.

- Once you leave, it is unwise to return.

- The chances the abuse will stop on its own are rare.

- Always have a plan B.

- Think about your own protection, even when times are good. That's not being negative; it's being realistic, and it's being smart. Everything is good when it is new, but what is your plan when or if your partner becomes violently frustrated with you? What is your plan when you are hit the first time? Think about these things long before they happen.

CHAPTER 8

HANDLING INCOMING AND OUTGOING MEDIA

Often individuals who attempt to perpetrate a scam or a fraud will likely solicit you in the one place you feel safe—your home. Whether it be by mail, phone, or door-to-door, they will make every effort to separate you from your cash on your own territory.

There seems to be an endless number of individuals who would seek to do this, but yet there is only one you. Unfortunately, this leaves you against all of those who are trying to get your money or your identity. When you think of it in that way, it can be a little overwhelming, but there is no need to panic. You can do simple things to secure your identity and your money from scammers.

Mail Security

Criminals commit fraud via the mail in several different ways, including the theft of your mail right out of your mailbox. They can mail you something that attempts to solicit money from you, or they can examine your mail to gain information as to your identity. No doubt your mailbox is inundated with all kinds of junk mail. In almost all of these letters is a request for—or offer of—money. These scams attempt to get you to send money for this or that. Some will entice you by saying that you have won some money—but must make a payment to cover fees to collect the whole amount. All of these types of mailings are scams and should not be entertained at all. The best practice upon receiving one is to proceed to the nearest trash can or fireplace and dispose of them.

From time to time, you may receive pre-approved credit card offers in the mail; generally these are exactly what they state they are. You get a letter in the mail that states you are pre-approved for a credit card. Also included is a short application that you fill out and send back if you desire to possess the card. Be especially careful with these. In the wrong hands, all a person needs to know is your full name, date of birth, and maybe your social security number, and they can send off for a card.

Any mail that you throw away with your name or any information on it should be shredded, torn to pieces, or otherwise rendered illegible. Identity thieves love to go through the trash of would-be victims, and whatever they find, they use. It may take several days of going through your trash, but if you are careless, they can figure out your whole name, date of birth, and social security number, depending on what you throw away.

The main thing is to maintain security of incoming mail; if you put it in the trash, make sure you render it illegible. It is recommended that you use a locking mailbox. These mailboxes are relatively inexpensive.

Here are a few things to remember when it comes to mail fraud:

- If it pressures you to act right away, be concerned.
- If it simply sounds too could to be true, it likely is.
- If it requires an upfront investment of some kind, it may be a scam.

Also be on alert for offers that:

- Promise unusually high reward for little to no effort.
- Promise instant winnings.
- Don't look legitimate.
- Just don't "feel right."

To expand on the last point, if it doesn't "feel right," that could be your biggest indicator that something is wrong. Less than 3 percent of identity theft actually occurs through the mail, but it does occur. If you suspect you have been a victim of mail fraud, you should contact the U.S. Postal Inspection Service. We have listed their information here for your convenience:

U.S. Postal Inspection Service
Criminal Investigations Service Center
ATTN: Mail Fraud
222 S. Riverside Plaza, Suite 1250
Chicago, IL 60606-6100
Phone: 1-877-876-2455
Postalinspectors.uspis.gov

You can also file a complaint with the Federal Trade Commission (1-877-FTC-HELP or *ftc.gov/complaint*). The FTC is the nation's consumer protection agency that works to prevent fraud and help consumers spot and avoid it.

Phone Fraud

The same concepts apply when someone attempts to solicit money from you via your phone in a fraudulent manner. There are several different types of scams through which a person can attempt to extract your money over the phone, but here are a few things to remember:

- Never give out any personal information over the phone to someone who called you.
- Don't participate in any surveys that ask you to reveal personal information about yourself.
- Don't key in any personal information on the touch pad of your phone at the request of a caller claiming to be a banking institution.
- Don't answer any questions to a caller who has not identified him- or herself.

The key thing to remember is when someone calls you on your personal phone, you have all the power and they have none. You can disconnect the call at any time. These callers rarely call back; they usually have a list of numbers in front of them, and when they can't scam you, they merely go to the next name on their list. It's a numbers game to them, and you are one of the numbers.

There are a number of charities and other business that legitimately call to attempt to solicit a donation or sell you something over the phone. These entities are not committing a crime when they call you, but if a caller makes you feel uncomfortable, go with your gut instinct and disconnect the call.

Door-to-Door Solicitation

Scammers who actually approach your home can be a little bit more intimidating, but the rules of thumb are the same. It is unwise to open the door to an individual you don't know. In this particular case, if you don't open your door to a potential scammer, they can't scam you. In the event you do, never let a stranger inside of your home, and again, do not give any personal information or answer any personal questions. If you are not interested, be polite but firm and end the conversation; there is nothing wrong with not wanting to spend your money or be scammed out of it.

Again, for obvious reasons, you should never open the door to an individual you don't know. It's better to be safe than sorry, and if you have a bad feeling about it, there may be good reason for it. If you do observe or come into contact with a door-to-door salesman, it may be totally legitimate, but for the protection of you and your neighbors, be sure to make note of anything that is suspicious. Take notice of the height and weight of an individual and what he is wearing and driving. You never know when such information may be material later on.

STRUCTURE SECURITY

Nothing that can be suggested or done can render a structure completely intruder-proof. Having said that, there are a multitude of things that can be done to make your home or business less attractive to criminals. The ideas that will be suggested here are based on the fact that most criminals do not want to be captured. With this in mind, it is our hope that you can discourage a would-be intruder and make him think of moving on to another target.

Ideally, you want to make yourself seem less vulnerable to a personal attack from an assailant, as we discussed in previous chapters. The same is true for your home or business; you want to make it seem less vulnerable to an attack. There are safety measures you can take that will cost you thousands if you have that to spend, and there are safety measures that just take a little labor and common sense; we will explore both.

On the less-costly/common-sense end, most of what is suggested will be based off of principles of crime prevention through environmental design, or CPTED:

"a multi-disciplinary approach to deterring criminal behavior through environmental design. CPTED strategies rely upon the ability to influence offender decisions that precede criminal acts. As of 2004, most implementations of CPTED occur solely within the built environment." (Jeffery 1971)

Again, these principles are generally used to discourage the criminal act, in hopes that the offender will move on to something more opportunistic. For this reason, let us start outside the house with some common suggestions and work our way inward.

Shrubbery

Shrubs, hedges, and small trees planted around your home enhance your home's appearance and can look very nice. The thing about this plant life that most people don't consider is that tall hedges and shrubbery provide excellent concealment for a criminal who may be looking to make forced entry into your home. Often hedges are around windows and doors as well. The criminal can simply hide behind these while he works on making entry. Depending on how tall your plant life is, even if someone rides by, they may not see what's happening behind the shrubbery.

Recommendations

Trim all plant life at least twenty inches away from all entrances to your home, including windows. Trim all trees and hedges that are right up against your home down at least six inches below first-floor window levels.

Fencing

Many people like privacy fences; you can relax in your backyard without concern of other people being able to view you or your family in the confines of your own outside space. Many people believe privacy fences look good and can potentially enhance the value of the home.

When thinking of fencing, consider that while a privacy fence affords you privacy, it can also protect a criminal who may jump that fence into your back yard. The criminal can have free rein to operate on your back doors and windows because no one will be able to see this activity.

Recommendations

If you must have a privacy fence (or neighborhood association rules require it), consider one that is less than six feet high. This way, there is some visibility for neighbors. Remember, in terms of crime prevention, nosy neighbors are good. Instead, consider a chain-link fence, because it will provide maximum visibility. Use nine-grade or heavier wire woven in less than three-inch grids. For homes, the fence should probably not exceed seven feet. For businesses, the fence can be much higher, and if possible, topped with some type of barbed wire if you feel it is necessary.

Lighting

Just like hedges and trees, sheer darkness can afford almost the same type of hiding for a criminal looking to do wrong to you. Often homes are not properly lit around doors, windows, and garages—all excellent places to hide. A lot has been made of what "properly lit" means. Let us say that an area is "properly lit" when you have full view of the target area and its surroundings from a safe distance.

So many times in so many neighborhoods, there is little to no street lighting. This can make the whole area dark, which is definitely something the perspective city or county you live in should look into, because it is a safety issue. However, this could take months, and you can't wait for government to make your home and family safe; you may need to act on your own.

Recommendations

In these cases, the most common suggestion is a simple motion-sensor light around the front door. Set the scan in a manner that it will activate itself upon detecting any movement around the front door. There are many different forms of lighting for your home. If you have the money, you can mount lights that stay on all night and turn themselves off automatically in the morning. And if these are affordable, by all means install them, but for limited cost in running and installation, motion lights are a reasonable solution. When there is no motion, these lights are off, saving you money until they are needed.

Alarms

Alarms should always be a consideration when securing your home; they are one of the best deterrents out there. If a thief or intruder attempts to enter your home and breaches the system, most alarms give out an audible sound that should bring immediate attention to the area. In addition, if the alarm system is monitored by an alarm company, police will be summoned immediately. A home alarm usually consists of at least one keypad, sensors, an enunciator (reporting device), backup battery, and an internal system microprocessor unique for each alarm company. There are many different types of alarms and alarm systems, but each system should be fashioned to the specific needs of the homeowner.

Any research you do will uncover more cases of times when an alarm actually helped someone than cases where the alarm failed them. As with anything, there are pros and cons to any system, and nothing is foolproof when it comes to preventing crime. Some of the cons include:

- *The system could fail to activate.* This is rare, but any system can fail, be bypassed or otherwise compromised. When house alarms were first installed in people's homes, many of them didn't have backup batteries. The system could be defeated by cutting the power to the home. For the most part this is no longer the case due to technological advancements.

- *Police response time could be slow.* Let's face it: the police answer alarm calls all day, among the many other tasks they have to perform. Most of these alarm calls are false alarms; therefore, generally an alarm call is considered a low-priority call in many police departments and may be categorized as such. In general, a call to an assault, homicide, or domestic battery may be dispatched before a simple alarm call. If you can't understand or agree with that, simply imagine yourself on the wrong end of one of those calls. Would you want the police to come to you first or answer the alarm call?

- *An alarm could cause the thief to panic.* There is a chance that instead of repelling a thief, the alarm could do just the opposite and make the thief panic, causing him to hurt someone, take hostages, or destroy additional property.

- *Cost.* It could be that the monthly cost of an alarm system just doesn't fit into your budget. There is usually a system to fit everyone, you may have to limit the scope of the alarm or the coverage, but you should be able to tailor the system to your needs.

Recommendations

Evaluate each alarm system you consider carefully, and check to see if the alarm company and system offer features that fit your needs. Alarm contacts that are placed on doors and windows should be placed strategically and wisely. Systems only come with a set amount of door and window contacts and a set amount of keypads. If you want or need more, they can be added at an extra charge. Window contacts should be placed along the back windows versus front windows, if you have to make the choice between the two. You should place the contacts on the windows that are out of plain sight, as that is where entry often takes place in burglaries. Keypads should be placed closest to the door you actually enter when you come home. For example, if your alarm is armed and you have to disarm it when you walk in the front door, you don't want to have to walk all the way back to your bedroom to the keypad to disarm it.

If the alarm package you purchase includes two keypads, you may want to place one at the door you enter and the other in your bedroom for ease and comfort.

Doors, Locks, and Windows

Another key part of your home defense is the doors and windows and the locks you put on them. There is no need to build a million-dollar house, only to secure it with hundred-dollar equipment. The weaker your doors and locks are, the better alarm system you need; the stronger your structure is, the less the alarm may come into play. For example, French doors are very nice looking and really enhance the appearance of a home. But because of the way they are constructed, they are a little easier to kick in than a conventional door, If you have these types of doors, you may need a more sophisticated alarm system or other backup since the door is easily defeated.

There is one thing that most people miss when talking about conventional doors. When a door is kicked in during a burglary, many times it is not the door that fails or gives—it is the frame around it that crumbles. One of the most important parts of the door is the strike plate. The strike plate is the part of the door frame that accepts the bolt from the lock. This strike plate should always be located adjacent to the stud in the wall. When the strike plate is mounted, the screws should be drilled through the strike plate, all the way into the stud at least two inches. The throw bolt from the lock should extend out at least an inch into the strike plate.

When it comes to doors, whatever the door is made of, it should be solidly constructed of that material. If it is a wooden door, then it needs to be solid wood; if it is fiberglass, it should not be a hollow-center door.

Adding a deadbolt lock to the normal locking knob is always a plus. The deadbolt should be of a good-quality single or double bolt that will lock out in the extended position.

Any windows can be broken if the thief has the time and determination to do so. Once they are broken, they are compromised. If you have a home alarm, a sensor should be mounted on the window through which the thief is likely to attempt entry. Another option is to place bars on the window as well, but this is a personal choice. As previously stated; bars may be very unattractive and take away from the value of a home. In addition, while intended to keep people out, bars could also keep occupants in the house in instances where there is a fire inside the residence.

CONCLUSION

It is our sincere hope that you have enjoyed this book and have been able to gain something from it that you may not have known or thought of before. What you have read is more of a practical approach to some issues we all face. First and foremost, they are the opinions of the author and how he sees it. The author gives certain facts that he believes support his point of view in some cases. This book is based on a living theory or idea of safety, rather than a hard and fast rule of safety and security. This idea is embraced simply because what may work for one individual may not work for another, and individuals cannot continue to make the same mistakes and expect a different result.

The truth is that people have to make hard choices for their own survival.

The truth is that all law enforcement agencies are not the same.

The truth is that people are often victimized by their own family members or friends.

These are truths that may sometimes be politically incorrect to say or write, but the author believes they are true just the same.

Out of the hundreds of burglary cases that the author of this book worked on when he was a police officer, well over half of these were committed by a suspect who knew or was related to the victim and not a complete stranger. The same can be statistically proven with little research when it comes to the abuse of children.

Lastly, if you know of a child or elderly person who is currently being abused, never hesitate to report it. You do a person no service at all by keeping something in the dark that should come to light. If you personally don't have the bravery to blow the whistle on abuse, make sure you alert someone who will.

THE CHILD/ADULT Safety COUNCIL
AND ADVISORY BOARD

JOHNNY FORD

CHARLA WOODRUFF

DEVONA ROGERS

SHANITA PARKER

KAREN DEMETRI EASTER

ALETIA BRADLEY-KNIGHTER

LAWANDA SMITH

ADVISORY

DR. CHARLOTTE WRIGHT

TAMEKA POLK, RN

WILLESHA NORMAN

Dr. Charlotte Wright

Education is a key component in keeping our children safe. As parents, educators, and adults, it is essential that we step up and talk with our children about the world that surrounds them. Failure to educate and communicate can have detrimental consequences. I am glad to see that Cory Harris is going take on a leadership role in the fight to protect our children, who are our future.

Dr. Charlotte Wright
Special education educator and advocate
Child/Adult Safety Advisory Board
Mother

Shanita Parker

As a woman entrenched deep in the faith and belief of our Lord and Savior, I look to the hills from which cometh my help for all things, including the protection of my children. The Word also teaches us of the futility of faith without works. For this reason, I believe in the use of common sense and prevention when it comes to our children as well as in our own adult lives. I have four children whom I love deeply, and I'm very active in their lives. I'm concerned about their safety, but due to my faith, I don't worry about it from minute to minute. I put all things into the hands of the Lord and pray for them daily. But when I get up off my knees and wonder what I can do for the practical application of my own as well as my children's safety, I look to true champions like Cory Harris.

Cory Harris has stared the worst of the worst in the face and brought them to justice time after time fearlessly. But even more importantly, he didn't just throw these evil men in jail, which was where they belonged, he took the time to extract valuable information from them in relation to why they do what they do, what drives them, and what was the origin of their evil. This took years and years of interviews and conversations with the most unsavory of characters. He has taken what he has learned and compiled it in one place to help us know warning signs, trends, and tendencies in other individuals we should take note of.

Armed with this knowledge, there is no telling how many children we can save if we are diligent and dedicated to get this message out. I will certainly do my part, and I'm proud to partner with Cory Harris and the Child Safety Council and Advisory Board.

Shanita Parker
Staff assistant, Prairie View A&M University
Child/Adult Safety Council Member
Mother

Aletia L. Knightner

I truly believe in the old adage, "our children are our future." I also believe it is everyone's responsibility to ensure that our youth of today receive the nurturing and protection that they need to develop into confident, well-rounded, productive citizens within our society. With that being said, I have made a personal commitment to do all I can for any child/youth who comes within my reach. Our youth need to know that they matter and that they can make a difference but it starts within themselves.

As a parent of two and a former early childhood educator and family assessment worker, I believe that the molding of any individual begins at home. However, in today's working society where both parents are working, or that single parent is working, our educators also play an important role in the lives of their students. Our school system should be a safe haven where our children are encouraged and given what is needed for them to exceed in society.

It brings such pleasure to know that Cory Harris has dedicated his time and devotion to keeping our children and community safe, and for that I sincerely commend him.

Aletia L. Knightner
Provider Service Representative
Child/Adult Safety Council Member
Mother

LaWanda Smith

We must preserve our greatest asset, our children. It is the responsibility of every adult to keep our children safe and in a healthy environment. In my professional experience (which includes working as a substitute teacher for one year in the Texarkana Arkansas Independent School District (TAISD), a post-secondary education in the business office for over ten years at the University of Arkansas at Hope, and my current work as a grant manager and a youth director for Court Appointed Special Advocates (CASA) for over five years), I have seen the adverse effects of abuse, as well as the emotional stability of children that dwell in a safe, healthy environment. Cory Harris's book puts the fundamentals of child safety forefront so that we as a community can more aggressively deal with this issue.

LaWanda Smith
HGT youth director and grant manager
CASA of Northeast Texas, Inc.

Willesha Norman

As a Family Service Worker for the Arkansas Department of Children and Family Services, I am responsible for providing protective foster care and supportive services for abused and neglected children.

Having worked on many of these types of cases has taught me the severity of child abuse and neglect. Statistics show that due to the Economic decline in America, the growing rate of child abuse and neglect has been rapidly on a rise. Many of the cases are based on drug and alcohol abuse.

Our goal is to provide secure child welfare and promote protection for the overall well-being of children and families.

Willesha Norman, Family Service Worker

Karen Demetri Easter

I work in the HIV/STD Hepatitis-C Section at the Arkansas Department of Health. I understand, as you do, that children are going to fall, and that being in abusive and neglectful circumstances is out of their control. What I want to discuss is a single preventable situation that unfortunately has many consequences and what I do to assist in its prevention. Sex! Young adults are having sex far more than those who are abstaining. As a matter of fact, abstinence is exactly the information that the education system wants promoted. That in itself is part of the problem. If a child has committed to abstaining from sex, their choice has one consequence: they will not have sexual experiences prior to marriage or adulthood before they are in a committed relationship. These are not the reasons for the HIV and AIDS cases that come across my desk. These abstaining teens are not the gonorrhea, Chlamydia, or syphilis cases that I see. Education is key to prevention

Practicing safe sex and being educated on things like the proper way to use a condom and making female contraceptives available is the way to vastly decrease the number of these preventable sexually transmitted, infectious diseases that are plaguing our youth. The Arkansas Department of Health is serious about education, prevention, and treatment. These are steps that are imperative to keeping the youth in our state healthy and free from disease. I follow up with physicians in seven counties to ensure that infected individuals have been treated, and I actively pursue those who have not. There is no greater joy than loving what you do, and every single day I leave my office knowing that I have played an active part in keeping the people in the state of Arkansas healthy and ensuring that someone will not transmit a preventable situation in our state.

I do not have children of my own. I have had eight nephews and three nieces with another happily on the way. I have beautiful goddaughters who are growing faster than I appreciate and many other children I take pride in knowing and having in my life. I follow what has been laid before my feet. I walk by faith and have love in my heart for all children and want to see them continue to grow and prosper in life, as many of us have been fortunate to.

Karen Demetri Easter
Disease intervention specialist administrator/budget specialist
Arkansas Department of Health, VCT Certified 2010
Child/Adult Safety Council Member

Johnny Ford

Our children are an integral part of the future of the United States of America. Adults must do more to provide a safe and prosperous environment for our nation's children. We must invest in the long-term future and growth of all children, regardless of race or creed. Children of today need guidance, mentorship, and nurturing more than ever. Education should be at the forefront and serve as the foundation which shapes their lives.

Johnny R. Ford Jr.
Senior Chief Petty Officer, United States Navy
Child/Adult Safety Council Member
Father

Devona Rogers

Our children are our future, and I believe we must do everything we can to keep them safe. We need to teach our children everything there is to know about safety, because this world has become extremely mean. It is our responsibility to empower our children with the right knowledge to keep them as safe as possible.

Devona Rogers
Child/Adult Safety Council Member
Mother

HELPFUL RESOURCES

Beyond Missing
www.beyondmissing.com/main.shtml

Child Watch of North America
www.childwatch.org

Child Quest International
www.childquest.org

Committee for Missing Children, Inc.
www.findthekids.com

Jacob Wetterling Resource Center
www.jwrc.org

Missing
www.usamissing.com

Morgan Nick Foundation
www.morgannick.com

National Missing and Unidentified Persons System
www.namus.gov

Family Watchdog
www.familywatchdog.us

ABOUT THE AUTHOR

CORY B. HARRIS

Cory B. Harris was born in Camden, Arkansas, and has over eighteen years of combined military and law-enforcement experience. He has served with the United States Air Force, Little Rock Police Department, United States Immigration and Customs Enforcement, and the United States Marshals Service. He has training and experience in field training, crime prevention, criminal and fugitive investigation and apprehension, operations, firearms instruction, threat investigations, and judicial and dignitary protection, just to name a few areas. He is also a recipient of the Medal of Merit (LRPD) and has a master's degree in criminal justice. This book is the second in the *Zipper Series* of law enforcement and safety books.

Personal message from the author

Thank you all for reading this book; just the fact that you have done so shows how much you really care for the safety of children as well as safety in general. In writing this book, I considered past and present issues and the consequences and outcomes of both. When you have been in law enforcement for as long as I have, it's hard not to notice things that seem to occur over and over again. I believe that if people simply have different information, they may act differently. No one sets out to be harmed, but things tend to happen contrary to what an individual may have wanted.

During my time in law enforcement, I have had the occasion to interview and speak to multiple suspects, as well as the victims of various crimes. Instead of just taking what was told to me as idle chatter to pass the time, I began to analyze what was said to me. I looked for common trends that occur over and over, and then I began to think of the best ways to combat or prevent them.

If something that is said in the pages of this book or through the words of the members of the Child/Adult Safety Council can inform a parent and enable them to save just one child, then I have done what I have set out to do. My faith and trust in God leads me to believe that it is my duty to do all I can, while I can. Although we all have different ways to contribute something positive to our society, we are encouraged in the Lord to be of help to our fellow man.

You can't put a price on your child's safety or well-being; a good parent would pay any price to prevent their pain if it were possible. You can't put a price on your own safety either, since your children depend on you to take care of them. I want to be the best parent I can be, and I know you do too. The good news I have to report is that through knowledge and lessons learned, you can prevent a lot of grief for you and your children, I'm proud to be a part of the solution through this book.

—Cory B. Harris, MS

ALSO BY CORY HARRIS

ZIPPER LE SERIES ONE:
Outlook on Leadership & Liability Issues in the Criminal Justice System **by Cory B. Harris**

- Published: May 2006
- Format: Perfect Bound Soft cover(B/W)
- Pages: 128
- Size: 6x9
- ISBN: 9781425907938

<u>OVERVIEW</u> FREE PREVIEW

The author takes you behind the scenes of the criminal justice system to bring you as close as possible to the mental reality required to be a police officer and administrator. In this book, he shares his experiences and that of others in law enforcement. These experiences all relay a message about what is right and wrong with the criminal justice system.

This book also explores various liability issues faced by criminal justice employees: racism, profiling, the thought patterns of law enforcement personnel, internal investigations, and more. Leadership virtues and what it takes to be a leader in law enforcement are also explored. The author is an expert in police/civilian relations and goes into detail about how mis-education can foster ill will between law enforcement agencies and the public. A must-read for pre-police officers, new officers, newly promoted supervisors, as well as civilians interested in the criminal justice system, there is definitely something here for everyone.

Zipper and this book are for sale wherever fine books are sold or at *www.authorhouse.com.*

REFERENCES

National Center for Missing & Exploited Children (2007) provided statistics—missing children, child exploitation, and number of children reported missing each year at *www.missingkids.com.*

U.S. Department of Justice, (2010) Office of Justice Programs, Office of Juvenile Justice and Delinquency Prevention.

United States Department of Justice. (1992) Justice Department National Survey of Crime Victims.

United States Department of Justice (2010) Dru Sjodin National Sex Offender Public Website, *http://www.nsopw.gov.*

City of Kenosha Police Department, (2008) Sex Offender Notification Facts. *www.kenoshapolice.com.*

U.S. Department of Transportation, (1995–2008) "Federal Aviation Administration; Unruly passenger statistics calendar years 1995–2008," Violations of 14 CFR 91.11,121.580 & 135.120.

Merriam-Webster 2010 Dictionary. http://www.dictionary.com.

Peden, M., Scurfield, R., Sleet, D., Mohan, D., Hyder, A. A., Jarawan, E., Mathers, C. World Health Organization, (2004) "World Report on Road Traffic Injury Prevention."

Holy Bible, King James Version (Proverbs 28:1), 2008.

Collins English Dictionary - Complete & Unabridged 10th Edition 2009 © William Collins Sons & Co. Ltd. 1979, 1986 © HarperCollins Publishers 1998, 2000, 2003, 2005, 2006, 2007, 2009

Sedlak, Andrea J, Finkelhor, David, Hammer, Heather, Schultz, Dana J, -U.S. Department of Justice. "National Estimates of Missing Children: An Overview" 2002 p.5
Jeffery, C. Ray "Crime prevention Through Environmental Design" 1971

www.ingramcontent.com/pod-product-compliance
Lightning Source LLC
Chambersburg PA
CBHW061733020426
42331CB00006B/1221